Coping with Miscarriage

Coping with Miscarriage

A Simple, Reassuring Guide to Emotional and Physical Healing

Mimi Luebbermann

Prima Publishing

PRIMA PUBLISHING and colophon are trademarks of Prima Communications, Inc.

Library of Congress Cataloging-in-Publication Data

Luebbermann, Mimi.
    Coping with miscarriage : a simple, reassuring guide to emotional and physical healing / Mimi Luebbermann.
      p.   cm.
    Includes index.
    ISBN 1-55958-503-X
    ISBN 0-7615-0436-2 (pbk.)
    1. Miscarriage—Popular works.   I. Title.
    RG648.L84   1994
    155.9'37—dc20   94-27377
                                             CIP

96 97 98 99 00 01 AA 10 9 8 7 6 5 4 3 2 1

Printed in the United States of America

How to Order:
Single copies may be ordered from Prima Publishing, P.O. Box 1260BK, Rocklin, CA 95677; telephone (916) 632-4400. Quantity discounts are also available. On your letterhead, include information concerning the intended use of the books and the number of books you wish to purchase.

Dedication

*To all those courageous mothers and fathers
who mourn the death of their unborn babies in
silent, and oftentimes, lonely grief. May we all
publicly acknowledge their heartbreaking loss
and dream with them of a future born with
healthy children.*

*For those to whom childbirth is denied, we wish
that they find the children who need them,
either through adoption or the role of listening
elder so missing in our culture today.*

Contents

Acknowledgments

This book started with the encouragement of Diane Stafanson, RN, who has dedicated her career to patients and students in the women's reproductive health care field and always made herself available to me for information and advice.

My sincere appreciation and heartfelt admiration for Barbara Barnes, RN, who created and continues to guide a miscarriage support group in Walnut Creek, California. Her sensitivity, kindness, and honesty have helped hundreds of women accept their miscarriage grief and go on to face each day and make the hard choices for themselves and their families.

Of course, this book would not have been possible without the welcome and acceptance of so many different women in the miscarriage group who shared their stories of pain and grief and their laughter and hopes for their futures. I thank also many friends and friends of friends who shared their miscarriage experiences with me.

Thanks also to those who have worked on the nuts and bolts of this book, from my agent, Martha Casselman, to Jennifer Basye of Prima Publishing, and Lisa Paul and Lynne Walker of Archetype Book Composition.

Introduction

The joyous news of pregnancy, whether announced by a doctor, nurse, or a color of the home testing kit, brings an instant sense of parenthood to mothers and fathers. Maybe you, the mother, already suspected a child was growing within you, needing you, depending on your protection. Suddenly decisions on what you eat, how you exercise, and when to go to bed become important. They are the first steps of nurturing and caring for your baby. You shimmer with the exultant glow, the warmth, the specialness of motherhood, and you sense the beginning of a great new adventure. For those women who know they are pregnant for even a week, and for those who feel their baby moving within, pregnancy is a glowing time of discovery, time for a sense of membership in the great human community, and for feeling blessed with the child growing inside you.

No wonder then that no matter how early in your pregnancy a miscarriage happens, the intense, searing grief you feel is the sorrow of a parent mourning a beloved child. The child is real; its death is the ending of hopes and dreams as final as any other death. However, grieving the death of an unborn baby is complicated by the invisi-

1

bility of the death. Because miscarriage is most often a hidden sorrow, sharing your grief with family members and friends may be difficult. To them, there was no baby, so the normal rituals of grieving do not apply. Yet without the rituals, the tragedy is minimized and parents often feel isolated and ignored.

Your aching emptiness is increased as your hormones readjust and your body heals, reverting to its pre-pregnancy state. Until your body regains balance, you feel emotionally on edge. These physical symptoms can be unsettling, and doctors and nurses are often not clear about the care you need to restore both your body and spirit. Nursing yourself back to mental and physical health takes time and effort, but launching too soon into your normal life to avoid the sorrow of loss can inhibit your recovery.

I became interested in women's health issues in the 1970s when I was beginning a family. My pregnancy ticked along so regularly that I rarely saw my doctor for more than a cursory check. At that time I felt ignored and slighted; now I know how lucky I was.

I became acutely aware of adolescent health issues while working with teenagers in a counseling setting. Because of this experience, I volunteered at Planned Parenthood in Oakland, California, as a pregnancy counselor. I worked primarily with adolescents, but also met many older women who talked about previously suffered miscarriages as they discussed family-planning options, health problems, or family size. Their grief seemed as fresh and raw as the day they experienced their loss. Natural feelings poured out, whether the miscarriage had occurred a month or five years earlier.

Although I work and write in other fields, I returned to the topic of miscarriage because I continue to meet women who live in emotional pain after losing a baby through miscarriage. At a miscarriage support group in Walnut Creek, California, during the last year, I met women who are silenced in their miscarriage grief as if they lived in some savage, primeval time. Frankly, I am outraged that women still wonder today if it is all right to grieve for their babies lost in miscarriage. Their babies died, and they must grieve to heal. My hope is that we can recognize these sorrows and stop stifling the natural pain these mothers feel, and instead respond with generous love and tireless support.

This book has been written to give those of you who grieve the facts and emotional markers to understand how miscarriage affects your life. The emotional trauma so encompasses the physical experience that it is difficult to separate what happened physically, and why it happened, from your feelings about it. By learning the medical terminology of miscarriage and understanding how you fit into the medical picture, you can begin sorting out your grief from your medical needs.

This book is for parents of all the diverse couplings of our culture, to men and women couples, for single women who have decided to become mothers even though they are not in a permanent relationship, for lesbian couples in loving, long-term relationships who can provide stable homes for children, and for infertile couples who must decide what their miscarriages mean to their goals of family.

Simply, it is written for all women who feel the quickening of life within them, and then, with a stunning river of blood, face the empty future of death. You need loving support, listening stillness, and educated knowledge to find your way back to life again.

Finding ways to grieve, ways to take care of your body, and ways to prepare for the future can make a difference in how you face life. Eventually, the body heals; intense, all-consuming grief diminishes. When you educate yourself about miscarriage and its grief, you and your family can mend together with a love that shares the future regardless of what the future brings.

To Fathers and Partners

You have just learned about your loved one's miscarriage and the death of your unborn child. Even if the pregnancy was in its first weeks, don't be surprised when you feel deeply disappointed and heartbroken that your child has died. Take some time to consider that you and the baby's mother lost a dream you shared for a future as a family. If the miscarriage became a medical emergency, and your partner almost died, you will feel angry, shocked, and then exhausted. In the following weeks, your loss will seem like a dull ache, and nightmarish panic feelings may sneak up on you in the middle of mundane activities.

Regardless of your pain, you will probably feel ready to reassume your normal schedule sooner than your partner. As you return to the comfort of your routine, you may find that you expect her to snap back at the same time. To your surprise, she takes a great deal longer. Even a year or more later, she may burst into tears. Give her time, hold her when she cries during diaper commercials or when she sees families with adorable babies. Her experience is naturally very different from yours, and her healing will take longer.

Women in America grow up expecting to be mothers. Often they delay childbirth, developing careers to better provide for their children. Regardless of their professional success, they want to produce beautiful bouncing babies with curls, cute clothes, and high IQs. Although these images are much like yours, the mother of your children, because she has primary responsibility for producing this scenario, has more invested in her success. Miscarriages are setbacks that touch a deep, socially cultivated self-image, and when that image is damaged, her whole being seems to be shaken with doubt and a sense of personal failure.

Besides her longing to create a family, she may experience intense physical symptoms from her childbearing. If the miscarriage happens early in the pregnancy, some of these symptoms will be minimized, but when a woman's body is ready to produce a baby, it turns into a machine churning out closely scheduled hormones. When a miscarriage occurs, the production is suddenly halted, then reversed. Closely akin to postpartum blues, this state affects her emotions. While she is healing physically, she must endure rebalancing her hormones, sometimes with terrifying symptoms of panic, despair, and intense anxiety. In time, her body will return to normal, but until that balance is restored, she must decipher life through a haze of hormones that can make her cry one moment and feel anxious the next. Do not minimize her despair or fault her for a less than instant recovery. Be prepared to comfort and support her. If she pretends everything is fine and does not attend to her grief and healing, she will take much longer to fully recover.

Even when things seem outwardly normal, when she feels like she is getting over everything, you may both get sideswiped with anniversary reactions. A woman who has miscarried has an internal clock that always, with a pang of regret, chimes the birthday of the child who was to be, and sometimes even marks the day she discovered her pregnancy, and almost always, the day she miscarried. Little things help on these days. Some women find comfort in lighting a candle, taking a walk together, setting aside some special time to remember the baby who died. When you share these times with her, you help her immeasurably as you strengthen your relationship. Sharing the grief makes it easier for both of you to bear.

You may be shocked when she cannot stand the sight of another pregnant woman, or that she feels intense anger toward women who bear children. She may refuse to go to family gatherings where well-intentioned relatives might blithely ask when she is going to start a family or, if they know about the miscarriage, might utter inane things about how losing the baby was "God's will." Baby showers may be tortuous events. She has a right to refuse to go regardless of her love for the person having the baby. You can bet she will explode when her parents tell her they want to spend Christmas or Hanukkah with the grandchildren, not with you and her because you don't have any kids.

Your job is to support your partner, to let her know her reactions are normal, and to encourage her to vent them aloud. Be her shield. Protect her as long as she needs to stay quietly at home. She will get out eventually, but forcing her to go places because people say it is good for her to get out may be unkind and unhelpful. If you feel her reactions are too paralyzing, and she seems too depressed after six months, suggest a follow-up visit to her doctor or contact a grief counselor for an appointment for both of you. Encourage her to go to a grief support group or a miscarriage support group where she can talk out her feelings with others who have shared the experience, who can cry and laugh with her.

When it is time to discuss having another baby, realize that the decision may be difficult. You may be ready before she is. Let her take the time she needs. The miscarriage leaves a wound that needs to heal; the time it takes is different for every woman.

Normal medical practice suggests a woman has a problem if she miscarries three times. At that point, her health care provider will generally suggest that a fertility specialist examine her and make recommendations. There is no reason she should wait out the excruciating experience of three miscarriages regardless of medical advice. After the first miscarriage, you can help her talk with the health professional about testing and other options to make the next pregnancy successful. The relationship between a woman and her health care provider often encourages her to be too passive, too dependent on his suggestions. As her medical advocate, you can actively research other options and support her in taking action to prevent another miscarriage. Almost every hospital has a medical library, and you can locate current articles on miscarriage to take to your health care provider for discussion of the newest medications and techniques. Working as a team, you can look to a future.

Above all, recognize that the physical and emotional trauma of a miscarriage can be a terrible stress on your relationship with your chosen life partner. When something as monumental as a miscarriage disrupts your plans and your goals, you come face to face with the depth and importance of your relationship with each other. Couples who turn to each other to help bear the load and make mutual decisions lay the foundation for a life-time relationship. Treasure and nurture that relationship, for strength from your mutual regard and affection will carry you through the difficulties of miscarriage, infertility, and other painful decisions that are part of life.

To Health Care Professionals

Of course, you are saddened to hear of a miscarriage in one of your families. But because you have many patients and see many miscarriages a year, it may not seem important to use your time with your patient and her partner to deal with the emotional and physical trauma of a miscarriage. Yet for a younger patient, this event may be the most catastrophic of her life and her first experience with death. For your mid-thirties patient, miscarriage may signal the end of her dream to become a mother.

Women who have miscarried are different from other surgery or obstetrical patients. You realize the agony that a miscarriage inflicts; you understand that mothers need information to cure their bodies and to provide comfort after the loss of their child. Mothers and fathers both grieve, but mothers usually grieve longer and more deeply. Women must cope with their personal loss, with anger that their bodies let them down, and with the possibility that they may never (or never again) produce children.

Miscarriage shatters dreams. Medical studies in your journals describe the lifelong emotional and physical consequences of miscarriage. When you announce the death of their child to the parents, realize that downplaying the state of the baby's development by calling it a "blighted ovum" does not help but confuses them. In their minds, the pregnancy holds a child, no matter how clinically small or large. They will grieve, no matter how long the length of the pregnancy. Talk to them privately in your office; grieve with them for a brief time, regardless of your schedule. With the unsympathetic social attitudes toward miscarriage that they will face, their time with you may spur their healthy recovery. Make sure you or one of your staff calls to check on them in a couple of days to be sure they are coping and recovering normally. Although it may be easier for you and your staff to sympathize with the parents of stillborns, studies confirm that parents of the very early fetus grieve deeply and need equal sympathy and understanding.

Women in America grow up with the social image of mothering children. For many young women, this death of their child may be the first time they have experienced the bleak finality of death. This experience, which may seem to you little more than a routine medical occurrence, can be a deeply traumatizing experience that requires years of recovery. For her the D & C (dilation and curettage) is a death knell, not a simple procedure to cleanse her uterus. She needs you to explain the procedure and to acknowledge her perspective. Women with intrauterine fetal death undergoing labor must not be left alone for long in the labor rooms. Before they go into labor, give them the choice of recovering in a surgical ward or an OB ward, complete with the crying of newborn babies.

If there is a stillborn delivery, deliver the baby into your arms as you would a live baby, for the parents can be disturbed to see their baby delivered any other way. Give your patient and the father the choice to see and hold their baby, wrapped in a blanket. Because many mothers may still be under the influence of anesthetic, talk to both parents before the procedure to make sure they understand their options.

Arrange to have a picture taken of the baby that the parents can look at when they are ready. Photograph the baby wrapped in a blanket, and save mementos for them such as a lock of hair or a baby footprint. Suggest they name the baby for the death certificate. Let the parents know the sex of the child. By letting the parents experience the death of their child, you are giving them the tools to heal from the trauma.

Talk to parents before a stillborn delivery about an autopsy; explain that this may determine what, if anything, was wrong and answer their painful questions. Let them know that the autopsy is a respectful procedure. Give them the choice to bury or cremate the baby's body. Suggest they bring in clothes for the child and hold a small private service, with or without the body. In their shock and grief, many people find these decisions too difficult to make instantly. Use your influence to make sure elemental details such as photographs and mementos are saved by hospital staff, and give the parents as much time as possible to decide on other issues.

For the follow-up appointment, do not usher these patients into rooms full of magazines with cheerful, round-cheeked babies on the covers. If possible, schedule their recovery visits after your normal hours so they do not have to watch pregnant women read parenting magazines in your waiting room. If this is not possible, have them immediately shown into a patient room, but first remove magazines that might cause more distress. Be sensitive to their agonizing pain and anger at the sight of women successfully carrying their pregnancies, while their own bodies have let them down.

Talk to them not only about their medical needs, but about the death of their baby. Encourage them to talk about what a family meant to them. When appropriate, let them know what their choices are in terms of their fertility future. Give them full information about what they need to do to heal their bodies. Slips of paper with admonitions of "pelvic rest" will not help. Explain carefully why they must let their bodies heal before trying again to become pregnant. If possible, introduce or recommend a hospital social worker or grief counselor to your patient. If such services are not available, call your patient at home at least once a week for several weeks to see how she is handling her grief and loss.

Test your patients to discover possible causes before they experience three miscarriages. Most women say that having a miscarriage becomes more difficult, not easier, with each successive one and their fear and anxiety increases, not decreases, until the process becomes almost more than they can bear. They deserve the choice of whether to risk another miscarriage or to be tested to determine whether there is any specific cause after the first miscarriage.

You may be able to heal your patient's body, but it may be harder to heal her emotional wounds. Miscarriage grief can be the source of prolonged and debilitating depression, particularly since miscarriage is often closely linked to fertility. Fertility issues reach the deepest part of feminine psyche, and unresolved feelings about miscarriage can haunt women throughout their lives.

Consider the value of offering miscarriage grief groups in your office, networking with other offices to reach women whose lives might be healed by sharing their stories. Ask patients who have successfully completed a difficult pregnancy whether they would provide phone support to patients with high-risk pregnancies. Studies show that patients benefit from the emotional support to talk them through the nerve-wracking anxiety that accompanies a pregnancy after a miscarriage.

Your patient and her partner may be deeply scarred from the miscarriage experience, from mourning the death of their child. Your consideration of their distress and your recognition of their loss will help them heal, in both mind and body.

1

How to Cope with the Grief of Losing Your Baby

Grief is numbing sadness
Grief is sobbing tears that won't stop falling
Grief is wanting to sleep and wake up to find it was
  a mistake
Grief is waking up to find nothing has changed
Grief is wanting to be alone
Grief is being lonely

You are pregnant. The tests confirm it, and you immediately tell everyone your exciting news. Soon your parents know, your best friend knows, your colleagues at work all know. Dinner conversation with the baby's father turns to clothes adorable on babies, favorite grandmothers, where to put the rocking chair, and of course baby names. Suddenly, you notice mothers pushing babies in strollers and pregnant women everywhere. You watch babies walk and talk, excited to think you too will soon be a mother.

And then something terrible, unthinkable, and unexpected begins. You start spotting, perhaps only slightly, just a brownish color. Nervously consulting your pregnancy books, you discover spotting is normal for many women in the first trimester, usually at the time your period would normally occur. You abstain from sex, thinking maybe that will help (it actually has no affect). You call your health care provider or maybe go straight to bed. But then comes light cramping, or perhaps even severe. Finally there is a gush of bright red blood, and you know the most terrible thing has happened. Your baby has died.

After that comes frantic calls to your medical office, probably a D & C (dilation and curettage), to make sure all fetal tissue is removed from the uterus to avoid infection, and then you are home alone again, this time all alone because your baby has died. But everyone tells you it was for the best, that something was wrong with "it" and you should feel relieved, you should feel happy, you should relax. You should just grin, take some aspirin, and bear it— and accept it as "God/Nature's" way.

Now you are confused and hurt. You thought you were going to be a mother. If you had a first trimester miscarriage (70% of all miscarriages), health care professionals may try to reassure you that it really wasn't a baby; perhaps you were told it was just a "blighted ovum." Your partner is relieved you are alive, and knowing you are, he wants to return to work and to normal life. You seem to be the only one who still cares, who can't stop crying, who misses the baby that was to be. Is there something wrong with you? Why does everyone expect you to bounce right back? Your body is telling you things are not back to normal, and your heart is breaking.

Miscarriage is the Death of Your Baby

One of the most difficult aspects of miscarriage is that, in your eyes, no one seems to understand that your baby died and that you feel totally different than before the death. You are the only one who seems to care that your baby lived and died. This intense feeling of being misunderstood adds to the pain and loneliness of grieving. Words such as "miscarriage," "fetus," or "blighted ovum" depersonalize the experience of being a mother, deny your yearning to hold and nurture your baby.

Regardless of all the advice, opinions, suggestions, and views, solicited or not, remember you have every right to mourn the death of your child. Do not let anyone deprive you of that tragic privilege of motherhood. There is nothing wrong with feeling numb and so achingly sad that you don't want to get out of bed, don't want to talk to anyone, don't want to go on with your daily routine. You are grieving, and that is how a grieving person feels.

You are not comforted when your family or friends tell you not to worry, it wasn't really a baby at all. Even qualified health professionals may not understand the complicated and intense feelings miscarriage leaves behind. They may play down the event out of a sense of misguided helpfulness. Trying to convince the patient that there was really no baby but only a cluster of malformed cells does an injustice to the mother who has a strong sense of attachment to her unborn child. Just because your baby was only 8 weeks when it died doesn't mean you loved it less than if it had been 18 weeks.

Fathers similarly may try to desensitize the miscarriage, to persuade their partners that it wasn't really so bad, that everything is really all right. In many cases, fathers experience miscarriage as a frightening medical emergency that threatens the life of someone they love above all others. Fathers often focus on their relief that the mother has survived. Sometimes they harbor unrecognized anger from their desperate fright and later feel resentment when their partner is not recovering from her miscarriage. Their joy that the mother survived sometimes makes fathers discount the death of the baby. Sometimes they purposely ignore the fact in order, so they think, to make the mother feel better.

Men have not experienced their body creating a baby, with the complex chemical changes and satisfying psychological and spiritual emotions. Also they relate to events differently than women do. They see a return to normal schedules as proof of their strength and manliness. They are often puzzled, frustrated, and then angry that you do not bounce back as soon as they have. When your grieving lingers, they can become impatient and hostile, putting a strain on your relationship at a time when you most need comfort and support.

Family members may never have experienced loss before. The loved ones you expect to be most understanding and most sympathetic may be the most awkward and say the most unhelpful things. "You are young yet, you have plenty of time, it didn't really matter." Such phrases from those you trust really hurt and make you feel all the more alone.

A Lonely Grief

In the twentieth century, when doctors and health professionals administer aid to a woman, often alone in a hospital, miscarriage has become a hidden grief. Each woman isolated by the medical procedure experiences her grief alone or with the father. Yet, the fact is that one out of every four pregnancies ends in miscarriage. With women delaying childbirth into their thirties, these statistics may increase. Of course, many women miscarry before they realize they are pregnant and other miscarriages go unreported. Consequently, the actual number may be larger.

If you have miscarried, you need to know that you are not alone in your grief. Miscarriage is much more prevalent than most people imagine, but again, the stigma of silence does the injustice of minimizing the problem and making women mistakenly feel they are part of a small group who fail to bring a baby to term.

Each parent will, in her or his own way, grieve for the lost child. Some mourn for weeks, some for months, and some for years. Parents feel public recognition of their grief is diminished because, in most cases, there is no body for a public ceremony. They endure glib clichés offered by their family and friends who mistakenly take their loss lightly. Although the comments are clumsy, albeit well-meaning attempts to be sympathetic, they often painfully underscore the lack of understanding about the grief of miscarriage.

Men usually find they can return to their routines fairly soon, although they continue to mourn. For women, miscarriage can be a major crisis that disrupts their life and plunges them into months of depression and sadness. There is nothing wrong with you if your feelings of grief do not disappear within a few weeks; many women take longer to recover.

Every Mother Feels Grief after the Death of Her Child

It does not matter how young the baby, how soon or how late in the pregnancy miscarriage occurred, but you will and you should grieve for your baby. You are not abnormal grieving for a pregnancy ending five weeks after conception, or three months, or just before delivery. Women react differently to their loss. Some feel it more deeply than others, but all women grieve after the death of their babies. Don't pay attention to anyone who says you shouldn't grieve for your baby. You are grieving because you had a baby and your baby died.

You may be confused about the symptoms of grief. For many young women, miscarriage is the first death they have ever experienced. Women are aware of a tumult of feelings, but they don't know if what they are feeling is grief. Remember, whatever you feel is appropriate. No one can say how long you will grieve or what specifically will help you—there are no guidelines except your own feelings. Some women feel they want to go back to work to be comforted by office routine as soon as they are physically able. Others want to be quiet and alone. Doing the laundry, going to work, getting dressed—all the things normally part of your day—may seem difficult or impossible to accomplish. The only rule in grieving is to allow the process to occur, because when grief is dammed up like a river, it eventually overflows, perhaps one, two, or even five years later.

When you are grieving, give yourself permission to be selfish. In our society, women must be the givers, the nurturers, and they seldom feel permitted to shut themselves away to take care of their own needs. When your baby dies, you will need time to recover. Try to arrange quiet time for yourself, refuse events you do not wish to participate in, don't take food to the potluck, let everyone else feed you, and don't return phone calls unless you really want to. You are grieving, and that gives you liberties that you would not ordinarily take. Take them now and let yourself heal. There will be other times when you can give back to those who help you now.

Single Mothers

More and more women in America are choosing to have babies without a partner. There are many reasons for this. Some women want children but have not yet found someone they want to share their life with. They know their fertile years are ending, and they want to go forward with their life goal regardless of their situation. Others find themselves pregnant when their couple relationship has broken up. Whatever the reason, these women find themselves doubly alone when their baby dies. This tragic ending of dreams and goals comes without the nurturing and support of a loving partner to help them through not only the daily tasks but also the pain and suffering of miscarriage.

Those of you in this situation may be very alone in your grief. Some women find their families and friends make no secret that they thought the pregnancy a mistake to start with and feel the miscarriage proved them correct. These people take cruel pleasure in belittling a single woman's desire for motherhood. If you are a single mother, it is even more important to find a support group you can depend on for sympathy and assistance during this time. You will need lots of help working through your grief, and when you cannot turn to family and friends, you can turn to those in the group who will give you the caring reassurance you need.

Multiple Deaths

Some women may suffer the death of a friend or a beloved family member just before or after they have their miscarriage. This death following so soon makes grieving doubly hard. If this happens to you, realize you are going to have a difficult time sorting out your feelings, and it may take you longer to feel better. As you begin to accept the first death, you will be thinking of the second death, and sometimes, it means you feel more intensely about both deaths. Be patient and understanding with yourself. You will be able to handle both deaths, but you may feel you are drowning in sadness.

The Process of Grief

Counselors who work with people in grief describe the recovery process in five stages. These stages are generalized, and you may find you sometimes feel all of them at one time, or you seem to go through mood swings that bring all stages in one day. They are described as shock, awareness of loss, withdrawal, healing, and then renewal. These descriptions are meant to give you a sense of reassurance that what you feel is a part of the grief process. If you don't fit neatly into the pattern, don't worry, because everyone has a different way of grieving. Grieving comes in waves, leaving you feeling submerged and overwhelmed one day and better the next.

Shock: "How Could This Happen to Me?"

Women who have had a miscarriage describe themselves as totally shocked it could ever happen to them. They assume their pregnancy will be normal, and having a miscarriage jolts them. Women who have had more than one miscarriage are equally jarred because knowing what to expect makes the miscarriage no less difficult to experience. Added to the mother's grief is her growing fear that she may never carry a baby full term. Women with three or more miscarriages find themselves diagnosed as "habitual aborters," an abhorent medical phrase that makes them feel worse about their situation.

The feeling of total numbness of shock and disbelief is the first stage of grief. You simply cannot believe that your baby died. Sometimes you must face this fact with your health care practitioner present; sometimes it is just you and the sonogram or ultrasound technician. There are times when you have gone to your appointment alone, assuming that it will be just another regular appointment, and then you must deal with the death alone, drive home alone, and wait to tell the father. This is a searingly painful time, each minute passing with excruciating slowness.

Many women are home alone when the miscarriage occurs. They fall into bed numbed and brokenhearted, often not thinking to call their health care professional until prompted by concerned family or friends. Many women are not sure how they endure the first day of their shock; they know only that it passes and they get up to face the next day. You cry and cry and cry, wanting never to stop. Tears fall at every small thing that happens from thinking about your baby to seeing someone else's toddler wobbling after her mother. Running out of your favorite jam at breakfast can cause a flood of tears.

Crying is the body's natural way of responding to grief. It is perfectly all right for you to cry, for crying releases your pain. Don't worry about other people's reactions to your tears or whether you are making them feel uncomfortable. Trying not to cry, stifling your sobs and tears seems to intensify the reaction, and instead of crying at home or in a quiet, private spot, you may find yourself weeping at the checkstand or in the middle of the train on your way home. Mothers who have miscarried cry; they cry a lot, and so they should.

The numbness gradually wears off over the weeks and months, but in the beginning, it can give you a sense of floating unreality, a feeling of being wrapped in cotton, a withdrawal from the world. Sounds may seem peculiar, too loud or too soft. People seem to mouth words you don't even hear. You may not want to move, but just sit quietly or lie in bed thinking of your baby.

Gradually, life does come back into focus. The anesthetic of shock lessens your pain at the time of the miscarriage, and in time, you return to a feeling the ground has stabilized under your feet again, and tasks don't seem quite so difficult; routine seems comforting and helpful.

Anger: "It's Not Fair; It Shouldn't Have Happened to Me!"

Your shock can be mixed with anger. Feeling shocked and angry is very much a part of the first stage of grieving. The "why me?" is particularly hard to answer when you were so careful to protect your baby. You may find yourself furious at your own body for not keeping your baby safe. You may be very angry at your health care practitioner for letting your baby die, and lastly, you may be angry at your partner for not being present when you found out, or, when he did find out, for not appearing to care about the baby as much as you did.

As the days pass, don't be surprised to discover that little things irritate you more. If your partner doesn't put his dishes in the dishwasher, you may be furious he is so inconsiderate. If you have children, their happy, wild tearing around the dining room table may cause you to raise your voice in an uncharacteristic way, to shriek that they must go to their rooms and that you hate them. If a salesperson seems to ignore you, you may step up and insist you be helped instantly or rudely stalk out of the store.

These things are not like you. Your anger seems white-hot, and it just rises inside of you before you can do anything about it. You have every right to be angry. You wanted a baby and were unable to have one. It is normal and natural that you are angry. The challenge is to control the anger so you don't turn it against yourself or those you love the most.

Ask a friend, a family member, your pastor, or a health professional for time to talk about your anger. Warn them that you are very upset, and ask them if they are willing to let you talk your anger out. Talking out your feelings is one of the best ways to vent them, and even though you may find it scary, try to say everything you are thinking. Give yourself permission to be very angry. If you want, write down the worst things you are thinking at first. Show yourself that nothing you say or do is as bad as you think it is. Remember, there is no harm in your feelings. You are only talking about your feelings, expressing them verbally. Mentally ill people act out their feelings and that is what makes them harmful.

Try to accept the fact you will be angry and irritable for some time after your baby died. Make your life as easy as possible for yourself. Don't shop when the store is most crowded. Have a friend pick you up after work so you don't have the pressure of commuter time traffic and crowds. Make a list of a limited number of things you want to accomplish each day and do just your list rather than trying to crowd in too many chores and activities. Minimize the stress in your life. Your anger will gradually diminish, and you will find yourself laughing rather than cursing the newsperson who tosses the morning paper in the tree.

Awareness of Loss

Realizing your baby is dead brings a devastating sense of loneliness and aching loss. Losing a baby makes you feel hollow, empty, alone. This sense of loss is like a lingering ache that never stops. You cannot forget: everything you see reminds you that your baby is gone. Wherever you look, there are reminders of the future you had planned with the baby.

Some women react to their loss by discarding or destroying anything that had to do with their baby. Try not to do this. If pictures of you in your first maternity dress are upsetting, seal them in an envelope and give them to a friend or mother-in-law to keep until later. Mementos from the hospital—a picture or a death certificate—may be too painful to look at now, but many mothers find themselves comforted months later by having something special to remember their baby by. Give yourself time to adjust to the loss. These feelings ease, and other parts of your life fill in again.

Don't blame the father if he doesn't recognize your acute sense of loss. You are highly sensitized to your loss because you were nurturing the baby in your body, and it is natural you would feel the absence more than he would. Try to let him know what you are feeling and that you will, in time, return to normal.

Withdrawal and Depression

At some point during the grieving process, you are going to collapse. You will probably have overwhelming exhaustion, and the future will look impossible. All the bad things you think will seem true, and there will seem to be no other choices.

You will imagine never being able to get pregnant again, or never giving birth to a healthy baby.

Nothing will ever be the same.

Your husband doesn't love you anymore and he is planning on leaving.

You are a failure; you can't do anything.

You will never have a family.

Life isn't worth living because you can't have a baby.

This is the proverbial rock bottom. You have worn out all your defenses and have absolutely nothing left. Women experience different phases of this feeling. Some women "crash" with exhaustion after the miscarriage and cry themselves to sleep. After several days in bed, they feel physically rested and move into what they assume is the next phase. They go back to work, but one mistake on a project they have been working on, one forgotten phone callback, or one mislaid paper sends them back to the despairing feeling that they are useless, that they cannot do anything right.

Other women find they just cannot do anything at all. They sit in one chair all day, perhaps staring at the television set but not seeing anything. They don't want to move, they don't want to talk, they don't want to do the laundry or cook the meals.

This total blankness is a part of the grieving process, and there is nothing you can do but to give in to the deadness of it. If you are tired, try to rest. If you can, make sure you get out at least once a day. Try not to stay totally indoors the whole time. Go for a walk, drive to town and buy a cup of coffee, or even go to a matinee with a neighbor. If you are back at the job, try to pace yourself carefully, working slowly and without pressure if possible.

At this stage, cocooning is essential. Do not go out to social engagements unless you really want to. Think of yourself as ill, recovering, but needing careful reconstitution. Stay home and wrap yourself in a blanket of your own control and your own feelings. Rent videos of funny movies, read trashy novels, just sit and look out at the view. Give yourself the permission to grieve.

Healing

Healing is a very slow process for some, and for others can happen more quickly. Think of yourself as a scrape that has to gradually close over. It takes time, but slowly, slowly, it does heal. Healing (see Chapter 3) is an active process when you begin to think about the future again, to feel you are in control of your life and have choices.

The most important part of healing is to recognize that you will continue to grieve while you are healing. You will have terrible down days when anytime anyone looks at you, tears stream down your face. That is okay. You know that you are healing when the word "tomorrow" has a somewhat auspicious, tantalizingly pleasant ring of faint promise. You are healing when you stop a moment after you take out the garbage to lean over and sniff a rose, to crush a mint leaf between your fingers, to notice the sunset. Note that you are not "healed," but have taken a step. You are on your way.

Don't be surprised that even as you heal, a mixture of stages seems to blind you at one point or another. Coming around a corner and seeing a woman breastfeeding can stop you in your tracks. Hearing a woman mention in casual conversation her child's birthday and realizing it is the day yours would have been born is bound to stop your conversation, and may choke you with tears.

Renewal

Slowly life begins to come back into focus. You may still have bad days, or burst into tears on the way to the work, but you are able to think about how you want to order your life, the choices you want to make. You find yourself interested in other people, willing to listen to their problems. You find yourself interested in your partner's life again and realize that you and he can share.

Normal Grief Reactions

Women going through the grief process sometimes feel out of control, even crazy. You may sometimes think you cannot make it through one more day. Here are some guidelines to reassure you that in your situation of intense stress, what you are experiencing is normal. These feelings are temporary, lasting from days to weeks, going away, and returning like a boomerang, but eventually they fade until they become a distant memory. You can expect the following physical and emotional symptoms:

- a feeling that your life has been turned upside down and will never be normal again

- remembering the worst moments of the miscarriage over and over, like a stuck tape
- a lonely feeling of numbing sadness
- an inability to make decisions
- physical symptoms such as heart flutters, headaches, aches and pains in the breast and arms, and overwhelming fatigue
- a passive acceptance of other people's choices.
- a conviction that you are "losing it," going crazy, getting totally "out of control"
- being unable to fall asleep or to stay asleep
- wanting food all day or not wanting to eat anything
- forgetting things, losing keys, missing appointments
- telling everyone you meet your story, over and over again
- avoiding old friends so you won't have to tell them what happened
- wanting to stay in bed all day, to ignore chores
- being unable to plan ahead

If you feel worried that your symptoms are persisting and you still seem to feel the same, ask your health care provider if he or she knows of other women who had miscarriages with whom you might talk. Or join a grief group, see a grief counselor, talk to your pastor, or contact one of the miscarriage support groups listed in the back of this book for a referral. Don't wait out your grief; share your feelings with other people who have had the same experience and understand what you are going through. Reaching out for help is the first step of recovery. You will find you are not alone.

Anger at the Father

Miscarriage grief can bring on confrontations between couples. Regardless of how deeply couples are committed to each other, the emotions stirred up by a miscarriage may put a strain on the relationship. Grief is experienced differently by each individual, and grieving is expressed in markedly different ways.

Besides the fact men and women express emotions differently, there are many other reasons why you won't understand your partner's feelings. Families have unique systems of expressing emotions, and they imprint these guidelines on all members. When you experience a different family culture, when your partner sends out signals that you can't interpret, you may have bumped up against tribal customs different from your own. In some families, difficult occasions mean the family comes together for a huge meal, laughing, talking, telling jokes. This is their nonverbal way of offering support. Perhaps in your family, people assumed the mourning person didn't want to talk to anyone and wrote polite little notes or sent sympathy cards. Like an interpreter encountering unknown vocabulary, you must be cautious in interpreting your partner's expressions of grief. He is grieving (even if he tells you he isn't), but in his own way, which will be different from your way.

Grieving is related to the attachment a person feels to the baby who died. Most women bond to the baby as soon as they learn they are pregnant. However, if the pregnancy isn't planned, it may take some time to get used to. Men tend to bond after seeing a sonogram or ultrasound, a visual picture of their baby. If a miscarriage occurs, fathers grieve; but they find it easier to put the miscarriage aside.

For them, going back to organized life and work helps them adjust.

Mothers take longer to grieve and to heal, and their continued sensitivity may not be understood by the father who longs to have everything back to normal. When his partner seems unable to fulfill that expectation, he will feel anxiety that he may express with anger. He may be unable to understand why you don't feel fine, why you need to continue participating in a grief group, why you refuse to go to office or family parties.

You need time to heal, time to cocoon, time to be released from the burden of daily responsibility. Your partner may think, as a way of making him feel safe and nurtured, that you should return to your normal relationship with him, to your duties, to the way things were before. Alas, things are different. You feel different, you are different, and although, after time, things may approximate the way they were before, they will never be the same. You have had a life experience that has touched and transformed you. Understand that the experience has probably not been as intense for your partner.

Because you are grieving, it is important that you find some way to put aside your anger at your partner when he seems insensitive. Your emotions are like a turbulent storm, and the two of you are navigators in an old-fashioned plane flying through the turbulence. You have no visibility, only the shakes and bumps of the surrounding storm. Many couples in miscarriage grief find themselves without a common goal, their hopes of starting a family dashed with the death of the baby. They become angry at each other, no longer sure that their futures match up.

Even though it seems a cliché, riding out this storm will make you a stronger couple.

Anger at Health Professionals

Insensitivity toward miscarriage is still a problem in the medical community. A woman depends on her health professional to guide her through her pregnancy, and when she miscarries, she may blame her medical care. Sometimes mothers of stillborn or miscarried babies are placed on wards filled with babies and new mothers. Some mothers prefer that, feeling they were mothers even though their babies didn't live. Other women are traumatized by the sounds of crying babies. The problem is that health care professionals often don't recognize the depth of grief and shock the women and their partners face and do not offer them a choice.

At the time of your miscarriage, you are stunned and helpless. You need the guidance of the medical community to help you through the experience. When they don't provide it, you may feel angry at them all, from the person at the front desk to the nurse on the recovery floor. Health care professionals may not have given you, the parents, the choice to hold your baby, even if it is a tiny, underdeveloped fetus. They may neglect to ask whether you would like a picture taken of the baby. These mementos may be meaningful later. If you feel you were mistreated during the miscarriage, talk to your health care professional. Keeping your feelings to yourself will only interfere with your relationship with your medical advisor, and you will need a lively, supportive relationship during your next pregnancy.

If you are experiencing a second pregnancy, you may be extremely anxious about the health of your unborn child. Normal lines of communication with health care professionals can become urgent daily phone calls which sometimes backfire, resulting in minimal rather than more support and a stressful rather than relaxed pregnancy. Without thoughtful and sensitive medical support, you may become painfully anxious, which affects relationships at home and at work.

Your Follow-up Visit: Health professionals are not well trained in grief therapy, and they have been slow to recognize the difficulties of couples who experience miscarriage, infertility, and stillbirth. To doctors, a miscarriage can represent a medical problem, not the death of a child. The waiting rooms of obstetricians may be filled wall to wall with cute, smiling babies and pregnant women waiting for weekly appointments.

Do not be alarmed if you dread seeing your health care professional, particularly if the doctor and the staff seem insensitive to your situation. When you call, ask for a first-in-the morning appointment, and let the receptionist know that you have had a miscarriage and find it difficult to be around pregnant women. This is a normal reaction and nothing to be ashamed of. When you make your appointment, ask that you be shown directly to a patient room. When you arrive, repeat your request. Stand up for yourself in a polite but firm voice. Remember, you will be raising consciousness for yourself and for other women in a similar situation.

If you talk to people who have undergone a serious medical situation, they will say they do not like to return to medical offices. If you hold your hand over the fire and it burns, you will be reluctant to repeat the experience. Talk to your partner about you feel about your medical treatment and bring up those feelings with your health care provider. Take a few moments before you go to your appointment to think about how you feel and try to understand those feelings. Accept that you feel anxious or weepy, that you dread going, that you do not want anyone poking or prodding you. You may feel like a failure for having a miscarriage; you may feel like you didn't react to save your baby when you should have; and you may feel angry at everyone in the medical office, resenting the apparent fact that no one takes you seriously.

Admitting these feelings, talking about them with your partner and your health care provider will help you to remove their sting. To give yourself the widest range of options for the future of your family, you must like and trust your health care provider. Finding the way to talk about your misgivings with her or him will allow you to develop a relationship of mutual trust and understanding, which can lead to your goal of producing a family, with all the experience and assistance modern medicine can provide if necessary.

Anger at Other Pregnant Women or Mothers

Expect to feel unusually sensitive to other pregnant women, to pictures of cute babies, to diaper commercials on television, to your family's comments on children or grandchildren. Bursting into tears at unexpected times or flaring up at a casually dropped comment are a part of the grief experience and not evidence of a woman out of control. You will, in time, be able to deal with these things, but for the moment, accept your sensitivity. When you have a choice, spare yourself additional grief by not going to gatherings which will be painful.

Anger at Your Body

Finding out just what went wrong can aid your healing process because miscarriage is a shattering event. A miscarriage should be clearly labeled "a life experience." As one of those events that forever changes your life, it adds a filter to your eyes. Suddenly nothing seems the same. You may view your body differently, as if it is a friend who suddenly turned against you. As do other people facing major illnesses, you will find that your anger at your body's failure colors your reactions to pregnant friends, parents, or in-laws who delight in grandparenthood, or toward siblings successfully producing children.

Some women find sex frightening, particularly when they associate sex with miscarriage. Although medical literature shows that having sex does not trigger miscarriage, women and couples may feel terrible guilt if they link lovemaking with a miscarriage. Women who have had a miscarriage may be overly fastidious in procuring contraceptives or forbidding sex until they feel absolutely secure. They may continue to use contraceptives for a long time to avoid pregnancy and subsequent miscarriage.

If you find yourself feeling differently about sex, discuss it with your partner and accept your new feelings as a result of a traumatic experience. As you recover both emotionally and physically from the miscarriage, you will regain your interest, pleasure, and comfort in lovemaking with your partner. If your fears seem to persist to the point that your partner is frustrated and angry, you may need to consult a professional counselor to talk over your feelings and conquer your fears.

Part of your anger at your body is a frustration that results from not knowing why you miscarried. Finding out what went wrong may be difficult. There are a number of miscarriages that never have their cause defined. If you collected some of the miscarriage fluids and had the contents analyzed, there may be some diagnostic opportunities to help you in pinpointing the cause. Later in the book you will read about the tests that may assist you in avoiding miscarriage. But at this stage, what you need most is time to recover.

Anger at Yourself Because of a Previous Abortion

There are times in life when you have to make very difficult decisions. Many young women find themselves pregnant at a time when it seems impossible to have a baby; consequently, they have an abortion. No woman undergoes an abortion casually, and sadness and remorse is a part of the healing process after abortion. If a woman later in life suffers a miscarriage, she may feel extremely guilty about her abortion. Some women cannot help the thought they were punished by losing the baby they wanted for having an abortion on the baby they didn't want.

If you are in this situation, try to accept your feelings and understand that there are several processes going on for you. First of all, any death has a resonance with the other deaths you have experienced in your life. If you have another miscarriage, you will find yourself mourning for the previous baby as well. This is normal.

Secondly, in the midst of death and grieving, you want to know why the miscarriage happened. Blaming it on yourself for your previous abortion seems to offer an explanation for a situation that most often has no discernible cause. Try to sort out your feelings of guilt from the real explanation of the physical cause of the miscarriage.

To blame the miscarriage on your previous abortion makes sense only if you want to make yourself feel bad. Try to be reasonable with yourself. You had to make a choice many years ago, and you made what you thought to be the best choice. And remember, many women with multiple abortions go on to have successful pregnancies.

Putting Away the Baby Clothes

Depending on how far along in the pregnancy you were, you may be faced with a nursery to put away. For most mothers, this task is one of the hardest they face. Wait until you feel you can face it. Take your time. If you feel someone's presence would be helpful, choose someone who understands your grief, and let yourself cry or laugh as you feel you need to. Don't ask someone who is going to be insensitive and make you feel silly or crazy. When you finish the job, you should feel satisfied that, although very difficult, you have surmounted another challenge and you are ready to face the future.

Children

If you have children, you need to talk to them about the death of the baby. Even small children have a way of picking up enough from adult conversations to understand that they were going to have a brother or sister. You will need to tell them very simply, "The baby died, and I am very sorry. It makes me feel sad."

Children may have felt angry and jealous that you were going to have another baby. They may have wished to themselves that the new baby would die. When it does, they may feel that they caused the death of the baby. Make sure you explain to your children that nothing they did caused the baby to die.

Children grieve, and when the household is upset, their feelings can be very much on the surface. They may start to act out their feelings, refusing to cooperate, to go to bed on time, to take a bath. Children who are upset will want more comfort than normal. They may want to stay in the same room with you constantly, making normal routine very difficult. When some children hear that their mother "lost" the baby, they become very worried that they may get lost too, and they don't want you out of their sight.

In a household where there is a lot of sadness, children can become worried, constantly asking you if you are okay, or if you are going to play with them or read them a story. If you are grieving, it may be difficult to respond to your other children. But remember that they need your attention and reassurance that you love them, and you will be okay even though the baby died.

Reassure them of your love with lots of touching, hugging, and holding. Let them cry, and tell them that crying is okay and that you feel like crying too. Let them know that after a while, everyone in the family will feel better although you will always miss the little baby that wasn't to be.

You may want to do something special with your children to mark the baby's death. Children can draw pictures and make cards for the baby. They can celebrate the baby's birthday with a cake. This kind of remembering makes a child feel secure after the insecurity of death. Helping your children process grief at a time when you want to hide out in your bedroom can make you feel like a juggler with too many balls. Working with your children will also help you heal. A family that works through their grief together will be a stronger unit, and your children will grow up to be adults who are not bowled over by the sudden accident of death and grief.

Grieving Women Need to Cocoon

If someone was ill with the flu, you would not expect them to hop out of bed to go on a bike ride. Alas, we do not recognize that a woman who has had a miscarriage has the right to make the same kinds of decisions to protect and heal herself. Friends will blithely invite you to a baby shower or christening party. Your own parents will invite you to a holiday season party and spend the whole time talking about how great it is to have grandchildren. Your best friend will call up to tell you she is pregnant for the fourth time.

For the time being, until you feel comfortable, protect yourself by cocooning at home or in environments with loving friends who understand. By giving yourself time and positive experiences, you will begin to heal. You know that any wound perpetually scraped will not heal, and that needs to be your guideline for decisionmaking. If anything reminds you painfully of your miscarriage, avoid it. Do not go to the baby shower, even if it is the staff party for your boss. Stay home over the holidays. You need to protect yourself until you feel ready and, in time, you will feel able to generously rejoice in other people's occasions.

Anniversary Reactions

As time passes, the nature of grieving changes. It becomes something manageable, something that doesn't stop you from laughing, from living, from looking forward to your life. You will never forget your baby, no matter what happens to you, and a pang of sadness may occur whenever you think about what you missed, but this feeling is not crippling. Another reaction can occur, however, seemingly just out of the blue.

Sometimes in the first year, and even unexpectedly in subsequent years, you may experience what is called an anniversary reaction. This can take place in several different ways. The first year you may find it very difficult to approach your baby's scheduled due date. The day looms ahead becoming all the more ominous the nearer it comes. In fact, you may feel increasingly depressed, and find yourself crying inexplicably just like you did after the baby's death.

Anniversary reactions can also occur on the day of conception and the actual day of miscarriage. Don't be afraid that your distressed feelings mean you are starting your grieiving process all over again; usually, after the day has passed, most women find a great sense of relief, as if they had passed through a barrier.

Many women find it helps to mark the day in a significant way. Planning something special, whether it is lighting and burning a candle all day, planting a tree or a flowering shrub, or even sending a small wooden boat covered with flowers down a stream, makes a special point of remembering your child with reverence. This may also be a good way to include the baby's father. He can participate in a specific way to dispell his feelings and to share the experience with you. The bonds from this shared experience can heal in many different ways.

Grief from Replacement Need

Sometimes women get pregnant after a beloved family member has died. In a way, the woman has found a replacement for someone important to her. In these cases, miscarriage brings a different pain, for not only has the baby been lost, but the connection to the special friend has also been lost. In such cases, it is important to understand that the grieving really concerns two losses, and that the pain is very deep.

Grieving is a Part of Life

The all-enveloping sadness of grieving eventually fades and you will find you are able to go back into your life again, with laughter, with hope, and with a sense of the future. The grieving process will take time, but remember, you are in control of your actions, not your feelings. Your feelings are your feelings, and although you can deny them, ignore them, and try to fool yourself about them, you have them, and they persist. There is nothing to be done but to note them and accept them.

Think of your feelings like a roaring river, rushing downstream. If you try to paddle up the river, you will never make it. Not fighting the flow, but accepting the ride downstream is the only way to win the fight. You still have a future, although it has altered, and you can still make choices to create the life you want.

Questions to Ask Yourself

1. Have I accepted my feelings of deep grief for the death of my baby?
2. Can I give myself time and space to grieve for my loss?
3. Do I feel so out of control or so sad that I should go to a grief counselor or therapist?

4. Do I want to go to this party, baby shower, or family celebration?

Actions to Take

1. Join a miscarriage or grief group.
2. Find a special family member or friend who will listen to your grief and your anger.
3. Plan a memorial for your baby, plant a special tree, work with the pastor for a church ceremony.

2

Dealing with Family, Friends, Workmates, and Strangers

*Your partner is the person you chose to be happy
and sad with
Your family loves you but may not know how to help
you
Your friends may be frightened by your grief
Your workmates may only want to get the job done
Strangers can offer only clichés*

Loneliness is part of the difficulty women have in recovering from a miscarriage. Miscarriage in America and other modern societies has not yet been widely recognized as a life-changing tragedy, and consequently does not bring social understanding, acceptance, and support as does the death of a young child whom friends and family have cuddled and loved. When a child dies, others share the grief with the parents. With a miscarriage, the couple often is left alone and unacknowledged in their bereavement.

If you miscarried, you may feel you should keep the heartbreaking pain of your loss to yourself because miscarriage is a subject no one talks about. You may assume you should silently grieve, and absorb and accept your painful loss. Embarrassed and sensing terrible failure, you may not be able to easily discuss or share your grief. When you tell someone you have had a miscarriage, you may find yourself rejected, ignored, or bullied into assuming a cheerfulness you do not feel. With such consequences, it is difficult to trust that someone will respond to you with sympathy and understanding or acknowledge your deep feelings of grief.

A Society Ill-Prepared to Accept Death

When you feel injured and vulnerable, it is critical that your feelings are accepted and your suffering validated. Alas, your family and friends may question the intensity or the duration of your grief. Women all over America find this lack of sympathy for their miscarriage experience, reflecting our twentieth-century American inability to respect the suffering death brings.

Unlike many so-called primitive societies in which families prepare the body for burial and hold the funeral at home, in our society, death is handled by paid strangers. Today, we feel frightened and awkward around death, and the solemn ceremonies conducted in churches or funeral homes are the only glancing contact most of us have. Comfort comes to those of us who don't want to show our feelings, through the formality of the ceremony, the stiff handling of feelings without much room for an outpouring of pain. Grief for most of us is a polite ritual.

Miscarriage in the New American Family

In the past, health practices had no medicines or techniques to prevent a threatened miscarriage, and once started, miscarriages were inevitable. But times were different then. Women bore children at an earlier age, and without birth control, births were more frequent. The society was inured to the inevitability of miscarriage, and for the younger, fertile women, the ease of a new pregnancy was compensation. Nineteenth century society set the attitude that unborn babies who died were of little real concern because death was familiar and the next pregnancy was simply a matter of time.

In the 1990s, childbearing has changed for most women. Since pregnancies can be planned, many women delay childbirth until they reach their thirties. Women who remarry after divorce often want to start another family with their new husbands. These women do not have many years left to bear children so each child has a unique preciousness, a particular importance. The biological clock for older would-be mothers is a walking time bomb, ready to explode their happiness, expectations, and life plans. Many women must face the excruciatingly painful fact that their own bodies can sabotage their planned happiness. In this context, miscarriage is a devastating ordeal with long-term emotional consequences.

Miscarriage for Infertile Couples

Social understanding of infertility has not advanced with the times. A surprising number of people in America have no comprehension of how serious and how widespread infertility problems are in young as well as middle-aged couples. The media touts miracle babies so there is general awareness of fertility treatments and their effectiveness. However, unless a close friend or relative confides that she is seeing a specialist for fertility problems, you many never know of the months of taking hormone drugs, painstakingly keeping ovulation charts, and waiting in agonizing suspense, wondering whether this month you will be pregnant.

On hearing of another's miscarriage, people often mouth phrases they heard when they were growing up, such as "you're young yet, you have more time," or "don't worry, you can always have another." Besides communicating insensitivity to the mother's grief, these phrases ignore the perilousness of the situation when a couple has been struggling for months, even years, to become pregnant. When a couple has undergone long periods of difficult medical treatment so the woman can become pregnant, a miscarriage seems to destroy their hopes of becoming parents.

For those of you who have worked so hard to have a baby, only to discover your dreams dashed by a miscarriage, try to understand that most people have absolutely no idea of the enormity of your problem, the impact this death has on your lives. If you feel isolated and lonely, take measures to clue in your special friends not only about this tragic event, but about the long process of becoming pregnant.

Don't Expect Understanding

When you have a miscarriage, the first thing you must prepare yourself for is a lack of empathy and understanding at a time when you really need the most help and support. This does not mean that your feelings are invalid, or that you don't have the right to grieve; it means that you must be prepared to handle the awkwardness of the people you know and love the most, plus a lot of unsolicited and unhelpful advice from casual friends and strangers. Remember, you are vulnerable in your grief, and little things have a great deal more meaning when you feel fragile and brittle.

Among the things to remember when you are grieving is that the question "how are you?" is a greeting, like "nice morning" and "good weather today"; it is *under no circumstances* a question. Even though you are tempted to look to strangers as safe receptacles for your feelings, resist the urge. Strangers' prosaic, clichéd responses will hurt you more than they will help.

Cocooning

Barbara Barnes, R.N., who runs a miscarriage support group in Walnut Creek, California, suggests that women who have had miscarriages consider cocooning as their prescription for recovery. As it poetically describes, this is your right to stay home to recover your social balance slowly, to give yourself time to grieve and to heal. If you have had a few brushes with insensitive friends or family, you will acknowledge the wisdom of this tactic.

Use survival tactics. Remind yourself that your feelings of grief are appropriate and, until you feel stronger, you must do whatever helps you. Don't go to social events such as the following if you anticipate they will be painful to you:

- baby showers
- christenings
- children's birthday parties
- ladies' luncheons where conversation focuses on the accomplishments of offspring
- family parties with your or your partner's siblings, their children, and your parents, or any combination of the above
- your own or your partner's business parties when you will be forced to make polite conversation with strangers

These events can be exceedingly painful, and bursting into tears or screaming savagely at someone's inappropriate remarks (although you may be totally justified) will get you into trouble. Going puts you into a no-win situation. Send a gift and stay home. Otherwise, be resigned to getting through awkward events by hating everyone there, or by escaping early and sitting in the car weeping hysterically. Attending these events is not worth it. Protect yourself. Grieving gives you the permission to cocoon, to stay home feeling safe and secure without the often prying and hurtful attention of insensitive people.

One woman says that when she knows she cannot attend a function, she simply calls and says she can't come. She doesn't make excuses, she doesn't white-lie, and she never elaborates. She simply says she is sorry she cannot attend and thanks the host for the invitation. Try it. Saying no will make you feel strong and making such choices will help you take control of your own life. Remember, after you say you are sorry you can't come, say no more. Hold out in silence. Don't feel you have to apologize and stammer through false excuses. Most hosts will accept your word with a polite demurral and hang up. Repeat your regrets to those who push you, saying just what you did the first time. You know it will be lovely, you are sorry but you are not able to attend. Thank you, and good-bye. Your firm tones will take care of the situation. When you hang up, congratulate yourself!

Dealing with Your Partner

Your partner loves you, and he wants the very best for you, but he may not understand your grief just as you may not understand his. People grieve in their own ways, in their own time, and for a longer or shorter period. The father may have had less chance to bond with his child; his participation was limited because the baby was not growing inside him.

In the process of healing, you go into your own feelings, withdrawing from the father because grief and healing is an individual, isolating process that no one else can accomplish for you. After some time, your partner may want you with him in ways that are difficult if you need more time to recover. If you are having trouble doing your daily chores or going to work, he will begin to worry that you are not recovering. He may try to bring you back to him. He may suggest going out to a social occasion, when you feel like cocooning at home, or suggest a trip to his family, whose comments seem gratingly insensitive to you.

Couples grieving have a difficult time communicating with each other. It is as if the airwaves between the man and the woman are fuzzy. No matter what one says to the other, it comes across as critical, painful, or inadequate—in short, as the wrong thing to say.

Grief and anger are closely linked. You are unbelievably sad and angry that you lost your child; he may be just as sad and angry that he lost his child. That anger, which is almost like a volcano that has to blow up, is easily vented against the person you love more than anyone else in the world.

Here are some examples of inappropriately vented anger. You can probably list your own!

- He looks at you funny. You assume he thinks you are fat and blow up at him.
- You forget to mail the phone bill. He accuses you of losing all touch with reality.
- You don't want to go to a company party. He fumes that you just have to get over this miscarriage right now.

You need to remember that you are in the midst of a painful and emotionally complicated healing process. All your emotional nerve endings are exposed and painfully sensitive like a raw and open wound. If you hear yourself saying "You never really wanted the baby, you never really loved me!" you know you are in the middle of post-miscarriage couple stress. Both of you need to recover, and that process takes time and mutual understanding.

Back off and give each other a bit of room. Don't judge each other or your relationship at this time.

Try to understand the motivation for your partner's actions. If your partner seems unconcerned, overly cheerful, or so maddeningly "up" that you want to throttle him, talk to him. Many partners think they can best support their mates by being in charge, seeming unfazed, and staying in control. They may feel opposite—heartbroken and grieving—but they are doing what they think will help you. Instead they may drive you crazy, make you think they don't care, or hurt you by their apparent insensitivity. They think you need them to be strong and manly.

Of course the opposite is true. You want him to cry with you. In fact, his efforts to mask his feelings, to appear "strong," can make him angry and resentful at you. "Here I am doing all the work, staying cheerful, and all she does is weep." Talking about your own feelings and asking him about his can help you both understand how the other is truly grieving. Not judging, not condemning the other because her or his grief doesn't seem as intense as yours can open both of you up to what you share together.

Fathers have different ways of trying to reach their partners when they grieve. Some men can not really understand the enormity of their partners feelings, but they achingly miss their active participation in the relationship, the little gestures that tell him you are close and loving to him.

Your partner may complain about things, whether mundane household tasks or disrupted schedules, that indicate life is not back to normal. From his perspective, once things return to their normal patterns, that means

you are fine again and will return to him. His goal is to restore the loving relationship in all its manifestations. He
doesn't understand how long it may take you to heal and
that, although you may feel fine one day, the next week
you may plunge back into depression and grief. Your up-
and-down emotions are like a yo-yo.

Often men try to reach women through sexual intimacy. If you are not ready for sex, sexual tension between
you and your partner can place additional strain on your
relationship. Or you may want the physical comfort of
holding, not sex, and he may misunderstand your needs. If
you use birth control because you don't want to become
pregnant yet, he may resent the interruption of condoms
or other contraceptive methods.

Fights over sex can be terribly damaging, and couples
in their grief and anger can lash out viciously at each other,
bringing up every past sexual misdeed in the relationship.
Call time-out on fights about sex. They are painful and destructive at a time when you both are emotionally frail.
Remember, you love each other deeply, and sex is a warm
and reassuring way to express your love. Explain to your
partner your sexual needs, whether they are to just hold
each other or to have very gentle sex or sex with birth control. If you and your partner are able to reach each other
on a new, deeper level of love and understanding, your
tragedy will have given you a reward that will last the rest
of your life.

Try to remember that you loved this man before the
catastrophic event of miscarriage, and look for ways to
reach out to him and restore healthy communication and
intimacy. If you find yourselves fighting and arguing, agree

to a time-out pact until you can resolve some feelings of grief and anger at your baby's death for yourself and for him. It is critical that you agree that for some time, even though you may not understand the other's feelings, you accept that he or she has the right to those feelings. Remember there is no right way to grieve.

Expect your partner to think you will recover in a snap. If you go to a grief counselor or a support group, he will expect you to come home "fixed." He will be surprised if you continue to attend for weeks or months and talk with other women or with a counselor. He will feel sensitive and defensive that you may be talking about him during those sessions.

Reassure him that for you, saying good-bye to your baby is taking longer, and that talking about the death with other women who have experienced miscarriage is reassuring and makes you feel better. Explain that the laughter and the crying is a part of most groups, and that the sensitivity of the members makes you feel like a whole person again.

If you have no way to help him understand your feelings, you may need couple counseling. Most men are resistant to counseling. Their outrage, shocked looks, or bullheaded remarks when you suggest you both could benefit from counseling comes because men are seldom comfortable with talking to a stranger about their innermost feelings. If he will not come with you, go by yourself for professional advice to help you work through your own grief and learn ways to reengage your partner.

Make the difficult holiday dates special steal-away times for you and your partner. Mother's Day, Father's

Day, Christmas, and Hanukkah can cause emotional set-backs after you have lost a baby. Plan an out-of-town trip, go camping, take long day-trips. If you plan ahead, you make it easy to refuse family invitations because "you already have plans." Use these special occasions away with your partner to spend quiet time together, to celebrate your special union.

Planning a Ceremony for Your Baby Together

Miscarriage usually comes so quickly and so unbidden that couples are not prepared to deal with details of a funeral or memorial service. If you have had a miscarriage early in the pregnancy, there may be no remains to bury. If miscarriage or stillbirth occurs later in pregnancy, you have the baby's body. However, many couples faced with their baby's death do not ask and are not given the option of keeping the body for a service. Due to the circumstances of their baby's death, couples may feel uncomfortable and fail to request a funeral for their child, particularly if medical care providers, family, and friends minimize the tragedy in a misplaced effort to console the parents.

You may have had a funeral, but for you, perhaps it was too public a ceremony. Planning a special event together with the baby's father can be a way for you to come together and share the grief you feel for your baby's death. Many women find this helps their partners get in touch with deeply felt emotions about the baby and their aspirations of becoming a father. Use the ceremony to put into perspective the importance of your lives as a couple making it an event that revolves around your love and respect for each other.

Like peeling skin, the numbness that makes you feel so separate and distant from your partner and your life will eventually go away. You may feel angry at your partner one day and friendly the next, but gradually you begin to see in him all the charming features that first drew you to him. You have the chance to fall in love with him all over again.

Dealing with Your Children

If you have had a miscarriage and have other children, their presence can be both a support and a burden. You will have to stick to some kind of schedule to provide for them, and that routine can help you get through the hours. However, children's insistent demands can be difficult when you need rest to physically recover, and when you need quiet time to reflect on what has happened to you.

You may find your patience level very short. It may become easy to yell angrily at your children when the television is too loud for you to nap, or when they quarrel or forget to do their chores. Do not feel guilty about planning some time for yourself every day for a few weeks after your miscarriage. Help your children learn the time-out concept. Explain to them that when kids or grown-ups become upset about things, they go to their room for time-out so they can feel better about things after a quiet rest. Reassure your children that your time-out doesn't mean you are angry at them, but that you are feeling sad and need to be by yourself until you feel better.

Even though it is an added expense, if you possibly can, hire a baby-sitter to pick up the children and take care of them for several hours a day. Rent video films or let the children watch a few hours of children's television on the weekends to give you added time to rest and recover. If at all possible, ask friends and family to baby sit to give yourself time alone every day. Even an hour sitting in a chair and listening to quiet music can provide a tremendous sense of peace and strength. When you are sufficiently recovered, you can resume the normal household schedule.

If you and your partner are stressed and irritable or are fighting with each other, for your child, the world turns upside down. You may have a child who begins to bedwet, have nightmares and sleep interruption, gets in fights at school, or is destructive at home. These are danger signals that your child is having problems coping with her or his feelings about the miscarriage or its affect on you and needs your attention and help.

Try to take special time with the child every day. Find books specially written for children on grief and dying, and take time to read them together every couple of nights. Hug and love your child. Your touch will reassure the child that he or she is still important to you and that you still love him or her regardless of your grief.

Make sure the people who spend time with your child every day know that there has been a death in the family so they can understand the behavior and provide extra support and loving encouragement. Relatives can fill in to provide extra loving attention to help your children adjust to the tragedy. These special people can give the additional sense of routine and normalcy that will reassure your child that life does go on. A few minutes rocking together in a chair, or a special hug and a box of cookies are the kind of magical prescription that makes a child happy.

If your child's disturbed behavior seems to persist, make sure to visit your pediatric health care provider to discuss how your child is reacting to the grief of the miscarriage and the family distress and mourning.

Dealing with Family and Friends Who Don't Understand

When you look to your family and friends, realize that they may not be up to helping you. Your miscarriage might be your peers' first brush with death, and they will feel stiff and unable to comfort you. Many of your family and friends may not have known you were expecting a baby. Because these people are not prepared for your bad news, they may be shocked into inappropriate behavior when they suddenly learn of your miscarriage. Your pain and anger may frighten them, and their polite, seemingly unfeeling or embarrassed responses may bring you an additional sense of shame.

Your grief is natural and appropriate; they just don't have the experience to accept it. They want to help you, they just feel inadequate because they don't know how. If these people mean a great deal to you, and you really want them to understand what you are going through, make the effort to educate them. Xerox articles or passages from this book that particularly crystallize your experience and give them to these friends. Ask them to read about it and tell them quite specifically what you need from them.

"I would like you to help me plant a tree for my baby."

"I really need someone who will just listen to me."

"Will you come with me to my first medical check-up? I don't think I can go back alone, and my partner will be gone on a business trip."

"Will you come with me on a walk? I am feeling so sad, and I know I will feel better with some exercise."

Oftentimes, your grief outlasts their offers of help, and they may become impatient, expecting you to bounce back long before you are ready. Like your partner, they want the best for you. It disturbs them that you are still grieving and in pain.

Unfortunately, because most people are so unsophisticated in understanding grief, they often try to jolt loved ones back into their old selves. Offering stern clichés about "bucking up" or "getting on with your life" makes these people feel they are helping you. But even family and friends do not have the right to invalidate your grief. Do not give their expressions of impatience any importance. You can be disappointed that they do not understand, but do avoid getting mad at yourself and feeling you have failed because you are still grieving. You will continue to grieve until you start to heal. No one has any influence over the timing of grief; their clucking at you to get better faster will not do a whit of good.

Remember family and friends come in different types of friendship intensity. We have very good friends, the ones we will keep in touch with all our lives; we have casual friends, the ones we are glad to see at parties and activities; and then we have acquaintances we nod at in meetings or groups. You need the comfort and support of your very good friends, so take the time to help them understand what the experience is like for you, and ask for their help. Understanding miscarriage grief is not that simple. Don't have great expectations that even good friends will understand how you are feeling.

Dealing with Your Family

Families are complex, and your feelings toward different family members are affected by your childhood, sibling rivalry, adult life styles, and by the partners introduced into the family group. Although the word "family" glows with sentimentality, we all know that we love some siblings more than others, may think the new in-laws are tacky, and may really resent the attention a parent pays to the new step-parent.

Family events for childless couples, particularly after a miscarriage, can be gratingly painful. It is natural for grandparents to be loving to their grandchildren and to proudly make comments about their growth, their brains, their beauty. Your brothers and sisters may be affectionate toward you but still self-absorbed in their lives and their jobs. The social nature of the event may make spontaneous feelings toward a grieving couple seem inappropriate in the public context.

For some couples, the tragedy of the miscarriage intensifies all the subtle feelings between the partner and the in-laws. Women may hear innuendoes of dissatisfaction from their mothers-in-law. Men may hear their fathers-in-law whisper, "He never was good enough for my daughter, and now look what happened." Such situations are to be avoided with a clear conscience when you are recovering from a miscarriage. There is no reason for you to go to a family gathering if you are going to feel bad, or in fact miserable. When you are feeling down and disheartened, a perfectly reasonable glance may seem like poisoned daggers. Wait for yourself to heal. Use your "no thank you" skills to firmly explain that you are not yet up to social occasions, not even family affairs.

If the event celebrates your partner's family and he wants to go, give him your full permission. His going is not a statement of disloyalty. He loves you, but has loyalties to his family that need not conflict with his position with you. He may also sense that he is unsure how to help you. Send him off freely.

Use the time while he is gone to indulge yourself in nurturing activities. Take a long, scented bath, arrange flowers, garden, read a book, browse through gift stores and buy something for yourself. On no account make a martyr of yourself and do chores that tire you or that make you angry because he is having fun while you are working. Whatever you are doing, stop before you are tired so you aren't exhausted and grumpy when he arrives home.

Dealing with Family and Friends Who Are Pregnant

Most women agree that among all the experiences they have during recovery, one of the most difficult is facing their friends and family members who are pregnant.

Mothers who have just had a miscarriage don't want to see pregnant women; they don't want to talk to them; they may hate them ferociously for still being pregnant. These feelings may well up in you, and if you are not prepared for them, they will can broadside you with their intensity.

Jealous feelings are much a part of the miscarriage process. If you are not used to these angry, mean-spirited feelings, it is probably because you have denied them in the past, for we all have mean feelings. There will be no ignoring these—wanting to physically punch strangers or women you love in the middle of their pregnant stomachs. You will be aghast that you hate your sister-in-law, whom you have, for the past six years, loved even more than your brother. Some women in second marriages who miscarry are overcome with jealousy when their daughter-in-law gives birth.

You are human, and human beings experience good, kind feelings and vicious, hateful, violent feelings. This mix is normal for all people. Most of us have strong enough character that we don't act on the mean feelings. It is perfectly normal for you to think about violence, to imagine yourself shoving someone down a flight of stairs. But you won't; trust yourself, you won't. Recognize the depth of your emotions, and know that you are a whole, real person. Disturbed individuals don't know the difference between right and wrong; but you are distressed by yours, which means you do.

The important thing is for you to avoid situations where you are forced to experience the raw hurt of seeing other pregnant women. When you feel stronger, you will notice pregnant women without the gut-wrenching hurt that hits you now. Protect yourself by staying away from family gatherings and events where you will be forced into a confrontation. Use the "no thank you" technique.

Asking for Help

Women are trained not to ask for help, but to suffer through things alone. Sometimes women punish themselves by pushing themselves to "do it all" after a tragedy, perhaps thinking that keeping busy will distract them, perhaps feeling they don't deserve help because their miscarriage makes them miserable failures. Neither is true. You will be in pain from this tragedy for some time, and miscarriage is a tragedy that happens, not something you are responsible for or that deserves punishment.

Try to reach out for help from your family and friends. They will look for clues as to how you are doing and will ask what they can do. If you rebuff them, say you are just fine, or try to convince yourself and them that you do not need their help during this ordeal, people may assume you are fine. But help can make you feel better, and feeling cared for and nurtured by those who love you can help the healing process.

After the miscarriage, family may come over to lend a hand with chores, errands, and other children. When they ask what they can do to help, don't be polite and demur. Give them a list. Here are some suggestions:

1. laundry washing and folding
2. grocery shopping
3. light housekeeping

4. taking care of your kids for a short time every day or on weekends to give you time to rest and be alone
5. after a funeral, writing thank-you notes
6. bringing casseroles that can be frozen for later use
7. taking you out to lunch
8. chauffeuring you to medical appointments
9. bringing a plant that together you can place in the garden in memory of the baby
10. giving you a gift certificate for a special dinner out for you and your partner

Dealing with Your Workmates

Going back to work is difficult on many different levels. You will have to deal with workmates, some who may have shared your excitement over the pregnancy and will honestly share your grief, and some who don't know you but may be curious about what happened. Lastly, you will have the strangers you must deal with professionally without letting their problems, demands, or worries get to you. Maintaining your professional manner when you are grieving is particularly demanding and exhausting.

However, the office routine and brisk impersonalism can also be a comfort, keeping you busy with your job demands, satisfying you with a sense of tasks completed. Getting your work done will help you realize the many different ways you contribute and can build your confidence at a time when you are feeling very low. Try not to overload yourself, and watch out for volunteering for more than you can possibly complete.

It is important for your grieving and healing that you give yourself as much time as possible before you go back to work. It may be possible to link your sick leave to your compassionate leave to give you more time to rest and recover before you take on the rigors of your job. Talk frankly to your boss or to the personnel manager about your miscarriage and discuss how much time you need before you return to work.

If you are almost out of sick leave, see if you can structure your work day so that you work part time when you first go back. Working in the morning will be easier if you know you can come home and rest in the afternoon. Get both friends and family to help with transportation so you can avoid being jostled and pushed getting on and off buses. When you are tired, this can tax your physical resources.

Ask family and friends to help you in the first weeks after the miscarriage by bringing well-balanced meals that are filled with fresh fruits, vegetables, and a main course. Take a good lunch with you to work, and bring extra juices to drink during the day. Try to minimize your intake of office coffee; bring decaffeinated coffee in a thermos if you need to. Drinking lots of coffee may make you jittery and high-strung when you need to stay calm and emotionally balanced.

Choose one of your most helpful office mates to be a "buddy" during the first few weeks. While your body is readjusting hormonally, you will have mood swings and may find things at work getting on your nerves. You cannot afford to blow up at customers, hang up on clients, or get angry at your boss, so take your "buddy" into your confidence and ask that she or he help you cope until you get back into the routine. If you have someone to turn to in a pinch, you will have a safety net under you if a problem arises.

Dealing with Strangers

Helpful strangers are more a myth than a reality. When you are grieving, the normal response is to talk out your grief. However, anyone who greets you with the "How are you?" mentioned before is not prepared to have you start crying. Your reactions are normal. Grieving people do burst into tears at awkward times; it is a part of the process. However, it can be embarrassing, and although strangers understand, they will feel constrained and seldom want to get involved. The coffee server has people in line behind you, and the bus driver has to be on schedule at the next stop.

Expect to be overwhelmed by sad feelings while you are grieving. If you find yourself fighting back tears when you are out of the house, go to a quiet place where you can let yourself cry alone and gradually come back to composure. Try not to stop up your tears. Letting them out will relieve you, but if you can cry privately rather than in front of strangers, you will feel more comfortable. If you are embarrassed and feel the need to explain your tears to strangers, try saying, "I am recovering from a death in the family and feel very sad much of the time." This allows them to understand your tears but does not make demands on them.

Here's a list to keep with you for your own comfort, or to pass out to family and friends.

- I am grieving for the death of my child. Do not belittle my grief, telling me that it wasn't really a baby, it wasn't right/normal/healthy. I have the right to mourn my beautiful baby.
- Don't say you can understand just what I am feeling. No one can understand just what another person is feeling.
- Don't compare mine with anyone else's experience to make me feel I am being inappropriate. My experience belongs to me, and I cannot compare my baby with anyone else's.
- Don't exhort me to get better faster, to stop grieving, to get on with my life. I would if I could, but I have control only over my actions, not my feelings.
- Help me to heal by letting me cry, tell you about the miscarriage, show you the picture of my beautiful baby.
- Help me to heal by taking care of the little things so I can rest and be quiet without the strains of everyday routine.
- Help me heal by listening to my story, passing the kleenex box when I need it.
- Help me to heal by not making any demands on me until I am stronger. Accept the fact that I know what I need to do right now.

Questions to Ask Yourself

1. Who do I want to see, and who do I not want to see?
2. What do I need from my partner, and what can I give to him?

3. How can my family and friends help me?
4. Do I want to go to this event or will it upset me?
5. Am I going to be able to return to work and do a good job?

Actions to Take

1. Make a list of specific chores your family and friends can help you with.
2. Make out a time schedule that gives you daily quiet time to yourself.
3. Ask your boss or personnel manager for the maximum amount of sick leave right away. Don't wait until replacing you with a temp becomes inconvenient for your workmates.

Stupid and Insensitive Things Friends, Family, and Strangers Say About Miscarriage

Start your own list of the worst things people say to you. Most women agree that, just when they think they have heard the most insensitive comment possible, someone tops it.

> At least you didn't get attached to it.
> Aren't you glad your baby is an angel now?
> Come see me and my kids and you'll feel better.
> Cheer up!
> Don't you want to hold my baby?
> Forget it, it must have been deformed.
> I know you have been ill, but can you babysit for me tonight?
> It was a blighted ovum.
> It was God's way.
> It was Nature's way of getting rid of bad babies.
> It wasn't really a baby yet.
> It's better this way—there was probably something wrong with it.
> Just have another one soon.
> Once you're pregnant again, you'll forget all about it.
> You're strong. You'll get over it.
> You can have another one. Start right away!
> You *have* to come to my baby shower.
> You probably didn't really want it.

You wouldn't want a baby that had something wrong
   with it, would you?
What are you worried about? You have other
   children.
You weren't married, you shouldn't have a baby.

3

Healing Yourself After a Miscarriage

Healing is taking back personal control for your life
Healing is finding beauty in your life
Healing is rediscovering the things that give you joy
Healing is starting to grow again
Healing is being comfortable with your failures and
*   successes*
Healing is appreciating the love other people have
*   for you*

Healing is regarded as a mystical concept because its roots have been so obscured by our technology-based modern medicine. In ancient times, when the physical aspects of healing were less understood, many spiritual ceremonies focused on healing. Shamans, healers, and medicine women and men were medical practitioners as well as psychologists, for, as has been long recognized, healing the body and healing the mind are two different processes requiring different skills. In primitive cultures, these medical care providers gave potions to heal the body and performed rituals to cure the non-physical symptoms, which they understood were also making their patient ill.

Women who have had miscarriages will tell you that modern medicine physically cures them, but healing the emotional pain of the miscarriage is a slower, grindingly difficult process. There are deep inner feelings about the death of your baby that you must touch and recognize before you begin the process of healing emotionally. Like a deep puncture wound that must heal from within, healing from miscarriage starts inside you. If you cover over the top by pretending you are "just fine," the wound doesn't heal, but can fester for years. Some women take as many as several years or more to recover from the trauma of a miscarriage. It may be only when they enter a grief group that they feel at last they are beginning to truly heal.

Grieving is giving yourself up to your feelings of loss. In the midst of grief, there is nothing but a dizzying vortex of numbness and shock. Grief is a passive state, and in fact is treated as such in many cultures. In the Jewish religion, the grieving family is not allowed to lift a finger for the first weeks. They are attended to by the whole community, who see to it that the bereaved have nothing to do but absorb the shock of a death. In many American households, family and friends drop off casseroles and condolences so a grieving household doesn't have to worry about meal preparation. Jewish and Catholic churches have annual remembrances of those loved ones who have died as a way to publicly embrace the mourners who are recognized as still grieving, still remembering their loss.

At some point after the death, you will feel a change. Healing is the midpoint at which you accept the death of your child enough to think about the rest of your life. You haven't stopped grieving—far from it—but you have emerged, as from a chrysalis, and you are beginning the process of returning to life. Healing begins the journey to accept the death and go on.

The old adage that "time heals all wounds" holds out the hope that sometime in the future you will feel a whole person again, and the painful experience of your miscarriage will not reduce you to raging tears or indecisiveness. Your healing may take months or years, but the important point is for you to note the moment when you think about the future; you will know then that you have begun to heal.

One morning you may get up, look outside, and think how beautiful the day looks; you have begun to heal. Or, you may look around your house and go outside to bring in flowers for the dining-room table; you have begun to heal. Calling to thank someone for his or her kindness to you means you are healing. Slowly, with small steps, you notice the world around you, you bring a cup of coffee to your partner, you feel like making the bed and doing the laundry. You ask a work colleague how her or his child's soccer team is doing. You are healing.

Healing is an active stage, a process you can take in steps to bring your life together again. Once convinced that you can heal yourself, you will begin the first steps to take control of your life again. The sense that you control your own destiny is one of the most important aspects of feeling good about your life and yourself, and provides the courage for you to start over again.

Reintroducing Personal Ritual

Ritual in older cultures helped those grieving from the loss of their loved ones to recover. In Asian cultures, there are altars to ancestors in every house. Within their own homes, women and men burn incense and candles in honor of their parents. We in modern America have diminished the importance of ritual in our lives. Beyond church and Thanksgiving, we rarely come together in a ritual that honors the most important moments of our lives. Birth, death, marriage, christening, and a few holidays are all we have left from the ancient traditions of marking the seasons, welcoming the harvest, embracing the hardships of winter, and celebrating the rebirth of spring. Historic cultures had rituals marking an entire lifetime celebrated throughout the community by family and friends. Life was remarked upon by ritual.

You may be embarrassed to bring your friends together for a private ceremony to celebrate your child's life and death, but you will find that the importance of sharing rituals for the very deepest moments of life will bring you comfort and a sense of renewal. Name your child. Even if you don't know the baby's sex, find a name you and the father like. Plan a memorial service to mark the death of your child, whether a private time for you and the father to plant a tree or a funeral and burial held with family and friends. Direct the ritual yourself with the advice and contributions of your family. Play music that means something special to you; write a ceremony that voices your hopes and dreams as a parent and your love for your child. A memorial ceremony can be a ritual that helps you accept your baby's death as permanent and final, a guidepost to your healing. Don't be embarrassed. You had a baby and it died. It is natural for you to mourn your loss.

Daily rituals can help as well. Take a quiet time for yourself every day, light a candle, and sit in front of it. Have a certain place you put flowers of remembrance. If you don't have a picture of your baby, draw a picture and decorate it with pressed flowers. Place a dish of potpourri near your candle, and stir it after you light the candle to smell its sweet fragrance. Some women feel a certain bird or butterfly seems to be the spirit of their baby, and whenever they see it, they feel comforted. These spiritual feelings may frighten you and convince you that you are, for sure, really losing it, but childlike feelings are a part of the healing process, perhaps because grief is so elemental.

Some women comfort themselves by carrying on silent conversations with their baby. When they go to bed at night, they tell the baby all the reasons they wanted to have it and how much they loved it. They sing a lullaby in their mind and, like watching a movie, see themselves tucking the baby in before turning out the light. This imaging restores some sad part of us, makes us at peace, and seems to send out a beacon of light in the darkness of grief.

One school of psychology counsels grief patients with the concept that everyone has a small child inside them, and loss and grief frightens that child. It makes sense that your psychological child will need love and reassurance, so let the child in yourself feel comforted by what may seem childish and ridiculous to you as an adult. It is a part of the healing process.

Some parents light a special memorial candle on the anniversary of their baby's death. Evonne Rand, at the Zen Retreat Center, Green Gulch Ranch, conducts ceremonies for miscarried babies and their parents outdoors in the beautiful flower garden. The family and friends of the baby write sayings and memories on beribboned slips of paper and hang them on the shrubs behind the outdoor altar. The papers looks like feathers gently blowing in the breeze.

In Japan, there is a candle ceremony for dead children, with parents lighting candles on little paper boats and letting them float down the river. Rituals are concrete ways to focus on our sadness, and once we do, these feelings are eased. If you don't want a public ceremony, make up a private one for you and the father. It is really astonishing how some very simple actions ease the pain of death.

Healing Your Body

Healing takes place in the mind and the body. Healing means you begin to feel like a whole person again physically and emotionally. You think about yourself, how you feel, how you look, and what you need to make you feel better. Begin by taking care of your body. Many women who have miscarriages are so angry at their loss that they turn these feelings against themselves as punishment for what they perceive, consciously or unconsciously, as their personal failure. They abuse their bodies by binge eating or not eating at all. Some women use alcohol or drugs, whether prescribed or not, as a narcotic against the pain. These gestures are like pounding your toe with a hammer so you don't feel the pain in your thumb. They don't work. In fact, they make you feel worse. Pain, unfortunately, is not swayed by diversionary tactics.

Take good care of your body. A careful diet of fresh fruit and vegetables, lots of water and juices, and a steady increase of exercise will make you feel good. If you want to lose weight, discuss it with your doctor, and work on a gradual weight loss program so you don't add a gnawing sense of deprivation to your post-miscarriage recovery.

Shortly after the miscarriage, your body will go through a transition state in which your hormones wildly fluctuate. Your physical healing has begun and your body will readjust its chemical balances, but don't be surprised or angry at yourself when you are hypersensitive beyond the bounds of reason. Don't worry about it, you are not going crazy—which is what most women think is happening to them—and as your body returns to normal, you will feel better. Worrying about your mood swings will only make you feel worse. When you begin to menstruate again, you will feel a sense of relief that at least a part of you has healed and returned to normal.

If you have gone through a labor or undergone a cesarean section, pay attention to and follow the doctor's orders. You want to prevent infections or other physical complications. The fatigue you feel is normal; it is the body's defensive technique to keep you quiet so your strength can be focused on healing. Give in to your fatigue and rest. Listen to your body's signals and accept the fact that you urgently need rest. Quiet resting has a way of healing body and soul.

Healing is taking good care of yourself. If you are working or have other children, finding ten minutes to be alone or to catnap in the afternoon is difficult. However, if you can manage to get help or to work only half or three-quarter time for several weeks after the miscarriage, healing will be a great deal easier.

People under stress do funny things to heal themselves. Some women clean closets and tidy dresser drawers; others cook themselves through their favorite cookbook or join a bicycling group. There is no right way to heal. Try different activities and continue to do what gives you pleasure. Feeling good is healing. At first, you will feel guilty about being happy because you will think it means you are forgetting your baby. You will never forget your baby, but you will think about the baby and your life differently as you continue to heal. Your loss will always be a part of you, but you will never again ache with such a mind-numbing pain. You will remember your loss, but it will not cripple you as it did at the first shocking realization.

In the initial stages of your recovery, keep things as simple for yourself as possible. Making dinner may seem overwhelming when you are stressed and physically strained, so have pizza delivered or pick up Chinese. In the short run take-out food may be more expensive, but these expenses are just a stop-gap measure. In the long run, you and your family will be happier and less tense. The house doesn't need cleaning every week. Bills do need to be paid, but you don't have to redecorate the guest bedroom unless that is really what would make you feel better. Try to sort out what must get done, and what you really can postpone until you and your partner are feeling normal again.

Forgiving Yourself and Others

After a miscarriage, you may feel angry at your body and weighed down by a terrible sense of failure. During your quiet times, think about this feeling of anger and failure, and listen to your feelings of incompetence. Many women hear an internal voice, or tape, that goes on and on about what they should have done to protect the baby, how they shouldn't have gone out that day, that they should have gone to see the doctor sooner, they should, they should. Imagine yourself as your own best friend, and gently argue back that there was nothing else you could do, that you did as much as anyone could. Forgive yourself and accept that you could have done nothing more. If you can forgive yourself, you begin to treat yourself more kindly.

Indulge yourself as you would a special friend who needs cheering up. Buy magazines or a fluffy novel you thought you never had time to read. Stop by the florist and purchase flowers to put next to your bed table, the kitchen sink, or your office. Take a soothing bath with fragrant bath salts; buy a new record and listen to it by yourself. Go to a funny movie and laugh all you can. Even better, rent a video and share it with your partner. Laughter is one of the great healers, and when you feel yourself laugh joyously for the first time, mark that occasion. It signals that you are making real progress.

Try also to forgive those people you love who don't seem to understand your grief and your needs. When someone you care about says something that hurts rather than heals you, forgive him or her in your mind by saying, "I forgive you for your ignorance, for your insensitivity." Relaxing your expectations of family and friends will help you relax your expectations of yourself. Letting yourself off the hook is another part of healing. No one is perfect, but your family and your friends do love you, and do want the best for you. You are deserving of their love.

Healing Through Keeping a Journal

Many women find it comforting to write down their feelings, their thoughts, and their dreams for the first month or longer after a miscarriage as a way to track their recovery. Although finding a moment of peace to write down what you are thinking may be difficult, it can be a useful healing tool. Try to use some of the quiet time you set aside for yourself to write.

Write anything. Don't worry about sentences. Start with single words or phrases. At first your writing will seem a jumble of scribbled bits—raging angry accusations at your body, sad descriptions of what you thought your life as a mother would be, fury at the medical world for not stopping the miscarriage. Keep writing down everything just as it comes to your mind. Try not to censor yourself. Obscenities, curses, all the worst things you think seem contained and safe when written down, flattened into one-dimensional lines on a piece of paper. Prove to yourself that you are still in control, that despite what thoughts you are thinking, they lie safe and sound on the paper.

Some women prefer to draw or paint. If that works better than writing, go right ahead. Or try making a collage by cutting up magazines with pictures of babies, rainbows, or rain clouds. Get yourself a glue stick, paper, and scissors, and then take the time to put it all together. You may start out feeling a bit foolish, but placing your hopes and fears on paper is healing. Include words as well if you like. Make sure to date every piece so, as you look back over them, you can see how your feelings change, how you begin to heal. Make pictures of babies for the gods, and burn them in the fireplace so the smoke goes up to the heavens. You may feel foolish doing these things, but you may also find yourself strangely comforted. Ritual has a way of reaching those feelings deep inside of us that we cannot admit or recognize.

Healing Through Talking About Your Feelings

Another effective way to heal is to talk about your grief. Of course, as has been mentioned earlier, in our society, miscarriage is not discussed in "polite company." If you find yourself talking about your miscarriage to people you don't know, from your seatmate on the bus to workmates to the teacher at your child's school, don't worry. Talking out grief is a healing process. The problem is that you may get bad advice or clichés from strangers that are more hurtful and irritating than helpful.

Look to your friends. Talk to them about your feelings, your despair, your anguish, and your guilt. Some friends will be unable to accept your pain and your grief, and you will quickly know you are making them uncomfortable. Don't judge them, and don't judge yourself for needing to talk about your experience. Not everyone has had life experiences to prepare them to share in the raw, naked grief of death.

If you can, find a grief group or a miscarriage group in your area and go regularly. In the company of women who have shared your experience, you can say whatever you feel. In their presence, you can lay out your deepest concerns and know you will be understood and not judged since these women have experienced the same thing. Heal yourself by going over the miscarriage experience again and again. Processing it helps you move back into the mainstream of your life from the side eddy of grief and loss.

Saying NO

Many women find that making time for themselves is one of the most difficult parts of healing. It is hard to avoid getting hooked back into the net of daily activities and social engagements before they are really ready. The word "yes" in response to a question seems to automatically slip out, but if you are recovering from a tragedy, to heal you must learn the word "no," practicing it in front of a mirror if you have to. Think of yourself as recovering from heart surgery, or an amputation, too ill to respond to everyone's demands. This metaphor for your condition should help you assess how seriously you must take your recovery, how responsible you must be for your healing. You cannot, just now, solve other people's problems. Simply tell them, "I am unable to help now, but I will call you as soon as I can."

Forging New Links

Sometimes when life deals you a terrible blow, you need to take on something new, a project you always toyed with, something to help you look to the future and break out of the past. Think about volunteering for a nonprofit organization. Try planting a garden, for growing things touches the need to nurture. Get four friends and start a book discussion group. Raise a puppy or a kitten, or bring home some goldfish. Try taking some adult education classes like a cooking class or a history of film class. Start a family genealogy, recording oral histories of your older relatives. Work with the local food bank to provide food for those without resources.

Working with other people in need can be a healing device. When you reach out to others, you bring a warm recognition of yourself as a person with skills and gifts, as someone who has something to give others in the midst of your own sadness. You realize that, although you have been baffled by miscarriage and childlessness, other people have equally distressing tragedies.

Coming Back Into Love

Grief isolates, but healing restores the bonds with those you love. Reach out to your partner, your family, and your friends. They will welcome you back gladly because they know you have been hurting but didn't know how to reach you. People are not instinctive about tragedy the way they are about happy occasions. You will notice that people whose lives have been filled with tragedy are most understanding of your situation. You may want to be grateful that your immediate circle of family and friends has not had enough practice in dealing with heartbreak to be helpful to you.

When Everyone Thinks You Should Be Back to Normal

Don't be surprised when the offers of help stop after a month or so, and everyone expects you to be back to normal. Take this as an indication of their regard for your emotional strength, and adopt a fall-back position. Continue to limit your activities strictly to conserve your strength. Try not to do too much, and program in extra time for yourself every day. Becoming angry and resentful that you cannot run your household as you did before the miscarriage is chastising yourself. Remember, as you heal, you will assume all these old roles; you just are not ready yet.

Lessons Learned

We don't think much about healing in this day and age, but you will need to learn much about it to restore yourself. As you pull yourself back into your world, you will find it is an exciting and fulfilling experience. Getting to know yourself better, and accepting yourself as you are will make you a stronger, more capable person for the rest of your life. Dealing with the death of your baby will make you a better, more conscientious parent, a better neighbor, and a more understanding human being.

Grief and death are as much a part of our experience as are joy and life. We all must practice recovery after tragedy whether it be the death of a child, a parent, a partner, or a sibling. As difficult as it may seem, we do improve as we go through life, probably because we understand the symptoms and we give ourselves permission to grieve.

As the old saying goes, the only thing that doesn't change is the existence of change itself. Disappointment and grief when our life plans do not work out as we drew them is as much a part of our existence as is the hope that next time, things will be better. You never planned on a miscarriage, but you survived the experience, and it toughened you for the rest of life. Knowing you have such strength should reassure you that you can take whatever lies ahead. That hope is what gets us through life, day by day.

Questions to Ask Yourself

1. Am I feeling ready to think about the future?
2. What do I need to do to heal my body?
3. What activities can I do for a regular exercise program?
4. What do I like to do for myself that makes me happy?

Actions to Take

1. Take ten minutes in the morning or evening to sit quietly and let your thoughts wash over you.
2. Start a journal, writing down all your thoughts for ten minutes a day or more.
3. Begin exercising every day.
4. Do something special for yourself every day.
5. Give yourself permission to chose only social events that will make you feel happy, not worried or upset.

4

Becoming Pregnant Again

Don't ever turn your back on your dream
Take each step one at a time
If at first you don't succeed, try try again
Remember we are all part of a larger family, and
*   many children need the love, attention, and help*
*   of an adult*

Women have different reactions to becoming pregnant again after they have miscarried. Some women want to become pregnant immediately, just to put the miscarriage experience behind them. Other women use oral contraceptives for years before considering the risk and trauma of another pregnancy. For women with fertility problems, a failed pregnancy may mean choosing a specialist to embark on a fertility program of drugs, or possibly in-vitro fertilization. Other couples begin the process of reexamining the options of adoption or choosing to remain a childless family.

Considering Becoming Pregnant Again

No matter how long you wait, you will find becoming pregnant again a different experience from the pregnancy that ended in miscarriage. Sorting out your hopes of having a successful pregnancy with your fears of experiencing another death can be stressful. Don't be surprised if you are excited at the prospect one day and anxious to the point of tears the next. These seesaw feelings are completely normal.

Just thinking about starting all over again can trigger feelings about the baby who died that you thought you had dismissed. You may find yourself crying at odd moments, feel that you are losing control, or find yourself frightened at the thought of slipping back into the kind of sadness you had just after your miscarriage. Some women feel anxious that, by trying again, they will forget the baby who died; they feel guilty about "replacing" the miscarried baby.

All these feelings are normal and are part of the grieving process. Recognizing them and admitting you are sad and anxious instead of denying these feelings will ease your worry and pain. Mothers who have had miscarriages always remark that they never forget their miscarried babies, but having a new baby changes the way they remember the experience. Notice that you respond differently to these feelings than you did just after your miscarriage. You are probably less paralyzed than when you were recovering and, although you are worried and anxious, the worry and anxiety don't take up all your thoughts.

Keep in mind that there is no magic time after your body heals to begin again, just the time when you decide as a couple that you are ready. This is not a decision to make lightly; you have the right to take all the time you need. If feelings of ambivalence about whether to have a baby or to wait longer threaten to overwhelm you, you aren't ready. If trying to make a decision within a reasonable time still upsets you, you will know you are not yet healed from your miscarriage. Wanting to become pregnant and being emotionally ready are not the same thing, and often do not happen at the same time. Look for a grief support group or a counselor and resolve your feelings first so you can approach your next pregnancy feeling strong and ready.

Being Ready as a Couple

Many couples have a hard time accepting how differently each partner copes with the miscarriage and the death of their baby. Your partner may think that the best way to help you deal with the death is to replace the baby with another pregnancy so he urges you to try right away. Or, he may be so distressed over the miscarriage that he doesn't want to consider a child and refuses to discuss the possibility until some vague time in the future. If he thinks you don't want a child, he may talk about adopting or remaining childless in an effort to comfort and support you. Or, in the characteristic way men communicate differently than women do, he may say nothing at all on the subject or suggest the miscarriage is in the past and should be forgotten.

If your miscarriage was a serious medical emergency, the father can be so traumatized by the experience of seeing his most beloved near death that the thought of subjecting you to another life-threatening pregnancy may be too scary to consider. Again, he may choose not to discuss the subject at all, or he may simply say he doesn't want to try again; the two of you have a great life and a strong relationship, you don't need children.

An event as momentous as a miscarriage can threaten the stability of a relationship and make the decision to have another child a serious issue between the mother and the father. Such an upset affects your lives like the distraught scribbles made by an earthquake recorder. Everything goes along within normal parameters and then the miscarriage, like an earthquake, causes the meter to go haywire. It takes some time after the earthquake and aftershocks for the recording to return to everyday patterns.

Imagine your relationship with your partner as constantly measured by an earthquake recorder. Try to let your relationship return to normal patterns before you make any big decisions. Deciding what to wear every day may seem too difficult while you are recovering; making decisions about a family while you are in your recovery phase is quantum leaps beyond that. The meter is likely to go berserk.

You may discover both of you have difficulty communicating your feelings calmly when you discuss having another baby and planning your future. Anger at each other while you are struggling to make up your minds about a new baby can overwhelm the decision-making process. Displacing your own pain by being angry at your partner becomes destructive to the relationship, the same one you cherished and desired before this tragedy. The expectation that your partner will understand your feelings and you will be sympathetic to his feelings is unrealistic.

No two people grieve alike. You may wonder why your partner doesn't cry, why he never talks about the baby. He may not mention the baby because he's afraid he will cry if he does, and he wants to be strong for you, thinking that is how he can help you. Validate each other's expressions of grief, and do not judge your partner by how deeply distressed you feel. If you have problems discussing the issue, that is a reliable sign that both of you need to take more time to heal before you start another pregnancy.

Sometimes one partner is ready for a baby before the other one is. Often, fathers are more optimistic and they are surprised at the mother's worries. Downplaying the possible problems in the next pregnancy seems natural to them, and they may try to diminish the pain of the previous miscarriage by reassuring the mother that she will have no problem with the next pregnancy. This can inflame the mother's anger, for it seems to her that the father is denying the importance of the baby who died. The father is surprised that his encouragement is met with the mother's fury, and he deems her unreasonable for holding on to her grief.

Lastly, if having a family is a long-term goal for both of you, reassessing that goal as a couple can make your relationship seem less permanent. Keep in mind that your primary relationship is between you and the father. Having children is based on your commitment to each other. Times of stress put unbelievable strains on a loving, intimate relationship. Remember that neither of you is wrong in your perceptions. You are like two people going up a staircase, seeing a different view depending on which step each of you is standing on. That doesn't make either person right or wrong, just in different places. You may want to seek professional guidance to sort out your hopes and fears about parenting from your feelings about each other.

Sex After Miscarriage to Become Pregnant

Trying to have a baby again means both members of the couple must be ready for a renewed sexual relationship. When sex becomes tied to making a baby, then loving intimacy often becomes tinged with overtones that can be confusing, particularly after a miscarriage. If you and your partner are having a hard time accepting the death of your baby, you may have trouble reinitiating your sexual relationship. Starting a dialogue about your parenting goals may help to unravel some of the emotional strands that block a sexual relationship that is intimate and loving as well as procreative.

Taking time out is essential to healing. You may have no problem returning to sexual intimacy, but if there are difficulties, talk about them with each other. If one of you feels the problem lies in trying to get pregnant too soon, use birth control until you both feel ready for a pregnancy. Start your intimacy slowly, recognizing the situation may call for staging romantic circumstances or an extra effort on each partner's part to restore special feelings of closeness. Most women feel comfortable having sex from four to six weeks after the miscarriage. If you find yourself uncomfortable with sex for a longer period, consider going to a grief counselor or talking with a therapist to help you recover from your grief.

Every couple must learn to face problems together; the reward is a deepening relationship with each other, earned from facing the hard lessons that life presents. Because miscarriage brings so much grief and suffering, your relationship may feel brittle and stressed. Finding your individual strengths when so tested and feeling the comfort of leaning on each other are great joys in a relationship. Indeed, one reason two individuals choose to become a couple is to have someone to lean on when life becomes difficult.

Family and Friends

Beware of family and friends who urge you to try immediately to replace the baby you just lost. They may tell you that "you'll feel much better being pregnant," that "you'll forget all about the lost baby when you have a new one." These comments are not helpful. In fact, they are often hurtful. You know you can never replace the baby who died, that she or he will always be remembered. In fact, having another before you have dealt with your grief for the baby you lost can be a barrier to bonding with your new child.

When someone you dearly love says things that do not validate your feelings, educate her or him on what you are feeling and the kind of support you need. Some women duplicate a special magazine or newspaper column about miscarriage that explains their feelings and give these articles to people who offer various clichés about "replacing" the baby through a new pregnancy. Your special family members and friends will be grateful to you for trusting them with your real feelings. By helping them understand, you will ally them with you, whereas your remaining silent may offend them.

You may need to place more distant family and casual friends on the "not worth the effort" list. Have a response planned when you are shocked by intrusive curiosity or unsolicited advice. Consider telling these family and friends, "Thank you for your concern. You'll be the first to know when we know anything." This script may not work for you, but make sure to devise one you can say even through clenched teeth. Practice it in front of a mirror before you go to a family gathering or social occasion. Be sure to put on a confident air that discourages further questions. Enjoy your power to quell their insensitive questions.

Trying Again

Just when you think you are ready, you may have days when you change your mind hour by hour. These conflicting feelings are normal after the distress of a miscarriage and, as you become more sure of your decision, you will gradually settle into resolve. Don't worry or get angry at yourself for being indecisive. You are facing a difficult decision and you need time to make it carefully.

If you want to try again immediately after your miscarriage, consult with your doctor. Most doctors recommend two to four full menstrual cycles after the miscarriage before you try to become pregnant. They make this recommendation to allow your body time to heal after the miscarriage and to return to the full working balance of hormones critical to normal egg production, a healthy uterus, and a menstrual lining able to support the implanted fertilized egg.

Women who have miscarried later in their pregnancy or delivered a stillborn baby may take even longer to return to their natural periods, sometimes as long as six to eight months. It may seem a long time to wait until your normal periods occur, but it is important that you feel confident you and your body are ready again. A woman recovering from surgery for an ectopic pregnancy has yet another time schedule. Even if you are very anxious to become pregnant, give your body the chance to return to its full health. Talk with your health care provider for a specific prescription on the time schedule appropriate for you. Trying too soon may well end in another disaster.

Use contraceptives such as condoms and foam or a diaphragm and foam to make sure you do not become pregnant until you are ready. Do not use oral contraceptives if you wish to become pregnant within the year because they interrupt the normal menstrual cycle. Your body takes time to readjust again after stopping them, possibly further delaying your pregnancy.

When you think you are ready to try again, consider your timing with regard to your miscarriage. If you become pregnant on your third cycle after the miscarriage, you will be delivering around the time you miscarried, an anniversary date that can be stressful. Some women prefer to plan their pregnancy to avoid any dates connected with the last pregnancy because they want to minimize any factors which might increase their anxiety. Anniversary dates such as the day you think you became pregnant, the day you found out you were pregnant, the day you miscarried, and the day you were to deliver are loaded with psychological explosives, and even if you think you can handle them, you may find yourself overwhelmed by a strong emotional reaction.

Trying Again for Women in Their Thirties

A woman in her thirties may be anxious to become pregnant as quickly as possible after her miscarriage, feeling that every month that passes diminishes her chances for motherhood. You may hear your biological clock ticking when you wake up worrying in the middle of the night. However, starting before your body and your emotions are ready will not put you ahead. If you don't take the time to assimilate the tragedy of your miscarriage, you may have more anxieties with your next pregnancy or problems bonding with the new baby.

Work closely with your health care professional. Explain to her or him your worries about becoming pregnant, and work together to come up with a list of realistic choices for yourself within a time schedule. Knowing your options and having a specific plan will make you feel more in charge of your life.

Here's the idea. A sample plan might give you a certain time limit to become pregnant naturally through intercourse with your partner. If you aren't pregnant by that time, you begin immediately with a fertility drug and vaginal insemination of your partner's sperm. After a prescribed number of months, you take the next step: in-vitro fertilization.

Of course, this is just an example. With your health care provider, you can tailor a plan to meet your own needs. Since methods such as in-vitro fertilization may mean additional costs, by working with your doctor to plan ahead, you can anticipate the costs and check with your health insurance plan to verify what procedures are covered and what you must pay for yourself.

Getting Ready

There are a number of important things you can do while you wait to become pregnant again. Take time to make sure you have healed emotionally from the death of your child. Find a miscarriage support group or a grief group (See references in the back of this book for national groups that can refer you to local members) and reach out to other women who have had the same experience you have. Working through your grief and learning about your feelings will help you deal with the normal heightened anxiety of carrying your next child.

Recent studies have demonstrated the importance of having a strong support group to contact throughout your next pregnancy. Establishing a phone network of people you can call for reassurance is an important part of planning to help you through your next pregnancy. Research has shown that mothers with high-risk pregnancies have a higher success rate in their pregnancies when they have a network of people they can check in with by phone on a weekly or even a daily basis. Sometimes your health care provider can offer this service or will help by referring you to past and present patients.

Your Health Care Provider and Your Support Team

Make sure you feel confident with the services of your health care provider and the support staff. Some women find they are angry at the medical team who cared for them during the miscarriage. You may feel your health care provider could have done something to prevent the miscarriage. Perhaps the staff seemed insensitive to your grief. The thought of going back to a clinic where you had a D & C may make you feel anxious and worried.

These concerns are normal. Talk with your health care provider about your feelings. Your provider must understand your anxiety, your problems, and your anger. She or he should work with you to improve the relationship. In most cases, there is nothing anyone can do to prevent a miscarriage. Asking your provider to explain your specific medical condition can help you understand why a certain medical response was taken. You need to feel confident that your health care team provides you with the very best medical care available for you and your baby.

If you cannot bring up your concerns with your medical provider, find another provider. Trusting this person and having free and open communication is essential to putting together a patient-medical professional partnership that can help bring you to full term with a healthy baby. Reassurance and good communication are critical to establishing a relationship that enables you to get the medical care you want and need.

Even if you prefer your health care provider, you may decide to consult with or switch to an infertility specialist or high risk specialist. If you seek assistance from a specialist, you may miss your relationship with your regular provider and wish to stay in contact. Also, since medical information can be technical and confusing, if asked, the specialist will often send test results to your provider who can interpret and discuss them with you if you prefer. Establish a relationship between the two providers that enables you to get the special information as well as emotional support and guidance. Because medical professionals are accustomed to consulting partnerships, they will not find your request unusual.

High Risk Care

Women who have had one miscarriage are at somewhat higher risk of having another one, and each subsequent

miscarriage increases the statistics. Current medical practice, however, is to wait for three miscarriages before taking elementary medical action such as testing to
determine the cause or causes of the miscarriages. Women
need not experience the pain and emotional distress of
three miscarriages. Instead, they can discuss their options
with their health care practitioners after the first miscarriage. Waiting for three miscarriages may not be in your
best medical interests. However, be aware that some insurance companies will not pay for certain diagnostic tests
until three pregnancy losses have occurred. You may
choose to pay for such procedures and tests yourself if you
and your health care professional decide they are worthwhile.

Some women, traumatized by their first miscarriage,
go straight to a high-risk specialist before they become
pregnant again. They go through several months of exten-
sive testing to eliminate many of the possible causes of
their previous miscarriage. They eat and exercise to bring
themselves to the best possible health and fitness, maxi-
mizing their chances of carrying a baby full-term. They
also learn all the symptoms of miscarriage so they can call
their health care providers with accurate descriptions of
the situation. These women know that they may still miscarry, and that perhaps nothing can stop the process, but
they feel prepared for another pregnancy as much as is
possible.

Follow the example of these women. Learn the danger signs that cue you to a potential problem with your
pregnancy so you can be confident in seeking medical intervention. If you have warning signals, there may be no

medical means to prevent the miscarriage; on the other hand, certain drugs or procedures might save the life of your baby.

Doctors Specializing in High Risk Pregnancies

Certain doctors called neo-natal specialists work with women to manage high-risk pregnancies and, as specialists, keep up to date on all the newest information on prenatal care that medical science has to offer. Ask your health care provider the names of local specialists for a consultation. If none is nearby, you might consider a trip to the nearest medical center for a consultation. You may not switch to the specialist for all your pregnancy care, but once she or he has examined you, you have the option of continuing to consult with the best trained professional for any problems that may occur during your pregnancy. If your specialist is not nearby, you can certainly continue your contact with weekly or monthly phone appointments.

Infertility Counseling

Some women cannot conceive without medical intervention. Their attempts to become a mother-to-be are like an Odyssean voyage, with obstacles at every turn. A fertility specialist knows the newest procedures and medicines to maximize the opportunities infertile women have to become pregnant. There are a variety of medical choices to help a couple become pregnant. Some are covered by

medical insurance; others are not. Before you start testing
or medical procedures, check to see what your insurance
considers reimbursable. Health insurance often does not
cover procedures the insurer defines as elective and, unfortunately and unfairly, many procedures vital to ensure a
pregnancy are so designated.

Many different organs are responsible for a woman's
conception, including the fallopian tubes, uterus, placenta,
and cervix. At the same time, a complex system of chemical reactions triggers physical responses. If you cannot
conceive, your doctor will begin a battery of tests to see if
there are specific physical problems which can be treated
with medical attention. Some tests are as simple as a blood
test; others require surgery.

However, conception is a two-person process. The father's sperm may be responsible for a couple's inability to
have children. The man could have a low grade infection
which lessens the amount of sperm available. In addition,
some sperm are not as lively; they lack the "motility" to
swim quickly through the vagina and the cervix, up the
uterus to the fallopian tube to penetrate an egg. Tests on a
sperm sample are relatively inexpensive and noninvasive,
and they are an appropriate starting place for infertility
testing.

Facing the Reality of Infertility

If you have had a number of miscarriages or cannot conceive for a year after a miscarriage, you may be facing the
fact that you or your partner has a fertility problem. This

can be a crushing blow to you both, and you may feel angry and depressed that such a thing could happen to you. Fertility is something that both men and women usually take for granted.

Unfortunately, delaying childbirth into a couple's thirties can affect the fertility of both the woman's egg and the man's sperm. Women facing the ticking of the biological clock may discover that their fertility was more limited by age than they had thought or imagined. Adjusting to a diagnosis of infertility is very, very tough, but be reassured that many infertile couples successfully become parents. Advances in modern medicine truly make miracles so that previously infertile couples are able to conceive and carry a baby full term. There is no reason to give up hope when you realize you are infertile.

Recognizing the problem can actually open doors for you. A number of excellent books on infertility are available. Educate yourself on the different procedures used to help to infertile couples. Although the process of taking drugs or having a laparoscopy to determine the health of your fallopian tubes may seem frightening now, you may never have to go to those lengths. Infertility specialists start with basic tests, and you may find the problem is as simple as an infection either you or your partner carries.

Many couples make the determined decision to try everything medically available before considering adoption or childlessness. Remember to take just one step at a time. If you are fully informed of the process and know what your choices are, you will find it easier to make the decisions as they come.

Preconception Care

Health care professionals are becoming more and more aware of just how important preconception care is to fertility and a healthy, full-term pregnancy. Talk to your health care professional about your previous miscarriage and ask what tests might diagnose the reason for the miscarriage. Remember, however, that after the miscarriage, there is often no way to diagnose what went wrong. You may never know exactly what went wrong.

Pelvic Inflammatory Diseases

Many women can carry a low-grade pelvic infection without any symptoms. Unfortunately, infections can scar the vagina, fallopian tubes, and the uterus, affecting your fertility. You will want to report any signs of infection to your medical care practitioner for treatment before you try to become pregnant again. Look for vaginal discharges unusual in color or quantity, itching around the labia, or discomfort when you urinate. Ask your medical practitioner for appropriate tests if you have these problems.

Rubella

Health officials thought that the population had been cured of rubella, or measles, but unfortunately the disease has reoccurred, probably because many children have not been inoculated. You can eliminate rubella as a possible cause for miscarriage by a blood screening. If you turn out to be susceptible, you will need an inoculation;

then you must wait at least two months before becoming pregnant.

Herpes

This very virulent, sexually transmitted virus has infected many women with painful sores that erupt periodically. Herpes can be very dangerous to the fetus in the womb and particularly during delivery. If you suspect you have herpes, tell your medical health care provider so she or he can watch for a flare-up and plan for your delivery so your baby will not be affected.

Hypertension

If you have hypertension, you may be on medication, some types of which can affect your fertility and cause miscarriage. Once your health care provider knows about your hypertension, she or he can prescribe appropriate medication which will not harm your baby. Hypertension that arises during pregnancy can signal critically serious problems with the fetus that require immediate medical attention. You may want to learn how to take your own blood pressure at home regularly. Swelling ankles can be an indication of a change in your blood pressure. Discuss this question with your provider so you know indications that signal danger.

Diabetes

Diabetes is a complicating factor for pregnant women, but it may not be a barrier to having children. You can also

develop diabetes during pregnancy. Question your relatives to see whether your family has any history of diabetes
and learn the symptoms. If you have diabetes, discuss how
this medical condition can affect you and learn how to
make sure you cope with the disease throughout your
pregnancy.

Genetic Counseling

Genetic counseling before you become pregnant may
alert you to genetic problems that you or you husband inherited from your family. Genes are passed down to you
through your parents, and everyone carries a variety of genetic abnormalities. When you and your partner create a
child, you are combining your sets of genes with their nor-
malities and abnormalities. Testing can alert you to any potential problems.

Immunological Problems

Our bodies are cleverly designed with a system that senses
illness attacking the body, whether the infection is caused
by an invasion of bacteria or viruses. One high-risk specialty is the examination of a woman's immune system to
determine how it may work to kill sperm or a fetus. Your
immune system comes with special blockers to protect the
fetus growing inside you. For some reason, some women's
bodies only recognize the fetus as a foreign agent and
do not produce the blocking antibodies that seal off the
baby cells from the mother's immune system. An
immunology reproductive specialist can test you for your
immune responses.

Diet

Increasing medical data focuses on the importance of diet in assisting a mother's body in regulating all the chemical processes that help form healthy babies free from birth defects. A recent study shows a connection between fetal neural tube defects and a mother's intake of folic acid *before* she becomes pregnant. The Centers for Disease Control and Prevention recommend 0.4 mg of folic acid per day. Folic acid foods include the dark green leafy vegetables such as chard, collard greens, and spinach, citrus fruits, whole wheat grains and breads, and dried beans. The Centers for Disease Control and Prevention see this link between the need for folic acid and birth defects as one of this century's most important medical discoveries to prevent birth defects.

When you plan your next pregnancy, ask your health care professional about starting your prenatal care vitamins right away to make sure your body is prepared for your next pregnancy through pills that provide generous vitamin and mineral supplements. Learn about basic nutrition, and eat lots of fresh fruits and vegetables, at least five servings a day. Work with your health care professional to be sure your diet meets all the requirements to get you ready for another pregnancy.

If you gained weight during your last pregnancy, you may think you have to go on a diet to get slim and trim before trying again. However, in light of the new study linking birth defects to poor nutrition, losing weight through stringent dieting or use of liquid diets may impede your chance of a new healthy pregnancy. Preconception fitness now seems to be essential to healthy babies that are free of defects. When you know you want to become pregnant again, make sure you check with your health care provider before you start a diet.

Your weight may be appropriate to your body type, but exercise will trim and slim you by working off fat and getting your muscles toned. So consider eating wisely and well, and just exercising rather than dieting. Try to work up to one-half hour of aerobic exercise every day. Maybe you can exercise to a video before you go to work in the morning, take a good brisk walk at lunch time (uphill if possible), or choose to walk up the stairs rather than ride the elevator. Start to improve your body through exercise any way you can.

Dental Care

Make an appointment to see your dentist. Have any X-rays and all your dental work completed before you get pregnant.

Alcohol, Caffeine, and Tobacco

Medical studies point to the consumption of alcohol, caffeine, and tobacco while pregnant as probable causes for defects that may result in miscarriage, so you may choose to discontinue these before you become pregnant again. If you are accustomed to drinking a pot of strong coffee in the morning while you are reading the paper, several glasses of wine at night, and cigarette smoking, you have a good project at hand to start cutting these three things out of your life. However, when you are under stress, stopping smoking can further upset you with the physical craving of nicotine withdrawal. If you stop having your morning cup of coffee, you can be hit with horrendous headaches. Relaxing with a glass of wine in the evening may be just the thing until your life gets more under control.

The point is that you do need to eliminate alcohol, caffeine, and tobacco, but do it sensibly and sensitively. If you are in a post-miscarriage state, you may already be stressed and depressed, and taking away any of these addictions will add a physical and emotional hardship. Begin gradually to change your habits, and enlist your health care provider and your partner to help you bring things under control. The key to a healthy withdrawal is moderation in the beginning. Make sure to include plenty of exercise in your daily routine, for exercise helps you feel better. As your body becomes more physically fit, your cravings will lessen. Exercising with your partner can begin to help both of you renew your relationship in a pleasurable, relaxing way.

Taking Part in Your Own Health Care

Before you become pregnant, educate yourself about different therapies prescribed for high-risk mothers. Almost every hospital has a medical library, where you can become an expert in treatments for miscarriage. The more you understand about your body's response to pregnancy, the more you will know what questions to ask and how to evaluate the answers. When you become pregnant, consider yourself your baby's best advocate.

Learn what signals your body might send to warn you of problems and what signs are a normal part of pregnancy. When something abnormal occurs, call your doctor immediately. If there is a problem, waiting may lead to a medical emergency. Know what your options are in regard to different strategies for high-risk mothers. If you are concerned about any aspect of your treatment, seek a second opinion. In the medical world, it is accepted practice to consult a specialist for advice, and your health care provider should welcome a consultation.

Enlist the father as a member of your medical team. The father can be your advocate. You might want him or another person close to you at your appointments to ask questions you might forget or not think of. He can also help you assess the situation and work with you and your health professional to plan a course of action. Knowing that you both are taking an active part in your health care can restore your sense of control. Knowing you did everything you possibly could in the case of a failed pregnancy lessens the normal feelings of regret and guilt afterward.

Tracking Your Ovulation Times

Ask your health care provider about tracking the time each month when you ovulate. When you are ready to become pregnant, you will have a record of your ovulation times, and you can more accurately predict when your body will be releasing an egg, increasing your chances of becoming pregnant right away.

The procedure is simple: merely take your temperature every morning just as soon as you wake up and record
the temperature on an ovulation chart, sometimes called a
basal body temperature (BBT) chart. It is important that
you are accurate so practice with a thermometer to make
sure you understand how to read it. If you use a thermometer that you must shake down, do so the night before. Insert the thermometer into your mouth the
moment you wake up, before any moving about, even getting up to go to the bathroom. Record what your temperature is after five minutes.

Your normal temperature should be 98.6°F, but your
body may slightly differ from this standard. Most women
ovulate fourteen days before their next menstruation, but
each women has her own schedule which can vary from
month to month depending on health, stress, and other
factors. Just before you ovulate your temperature will drop
and then rise sharply at the time of ovulation. If your temperature rises from 0.4 to 0.6 degree or more from one
morning to the next, you have probably ovulated.

Because each woman's body is so unique and some
women's temperatures don't seem to follow the rules, the
charts don't work for everyone. Try the charts out for
several months to see if you can document your cycle.
Remember, if you are trying to become pregnant just after
a miscarriage, it may take your body several months, with
two probably a minimum, to return to normal. Still,
recording your temperature is a way to start getting in
touch with your body.

Once you have ovulated, you will be fertile that day.
Most experts recommend sex every other day at the time

of ovulation to maximize your chances to become pregnant. This way, your partner's ejaculation has the maximum number of sperm and will be present in the genital tract.

For some couples, the BBT charts become a nightmare of programmed sex on demand. Some men resent having to have sex because the chart says it is time and, for couples, this issue of sex because a thermometer says "go" can become a battle. Take the time to talk out this problem with each other. Couples having fertility problems will need to discuss this issue and mutually decide how to balance their goal of following all recommendations for becoming pregnant with their natural equation for sexual intimacy. All couples undergoing fertility treatments will acknowledge what a strain sexual intimacy can become when trying to have a baby.

Being Pregnant After a Miscarriage

Women who have had a miscarriage find being pregnant again both wonderfully exhilarating and the source of overwhelming anxiety. Despite the reassurances of health care professionals, their partners, or even another high-risk mother, a pregnant woman who has had a miscarriage is going to be anxious she will have another miscarriage.

If you have had a pregnancy which terminated in a miscarriage, of course you will worry that your next pregnancy will also result in miscarriage. This fear is normal. The problem arises if you think your worrying is unusual—it isn't. Of course, it is natural for you to be concerned, but do not obsess about your worry. Carry on the best you can, taking care to make and meet your pre-natal appointments, to eat well—don't skip meals—get exercise, and rest regularly. You can continue to have sex with your partner; all the studies show that sexual intimacy relaxes you and, if you are having a normal pregnancy, it will not affect the fetus.

You will find that you are going to worry more when you approach the stage of pregnancy when you had your previous miscarriage. Women who have an undiagnosed medical problem may miscarry at about the same time as before, which is why it is important to work closely with your medical team to eliminate as many reasons as possible for a recurrent miscarriage.

When you come close to the time you previously miscarried, discuss your fears with your health care provider, and make sure that everyone in the medical office is alerted to the fact that this is a dangerous time for you. Ask your medical team what possible problems might arise and what their early warning signals are; then set up a plan with your provider if you begin to experience symptoms that cause you any worry.

If the worst happens and you do miscarry, be sure to save all the tissue that you miscarry. If you miscarry into a toilet, do not flush, but retrieve any tissue with a fine-meshed kitchen sieve. Place all the conception products you can collect into a clean container or a plastic bag. Call the hospital right away and let them know you are coming in with the sample. Make sure to ask them to run a genetic test on the sample; if you have a genetic abnormality, it will show up. This chromosomal diagnosis is expensive, but often it helps to pinpoint why you had another miscarriage.

If you miscarry again, you may feel like the ground has opened up beneath you. It was bad enough the first or second time, but another miscarriage comes with an increasing sense of despair that you will never be able to carry a baby full term. In your desperation, your disappointment in your body, your partner, and your life may be pitched to a level that makes you feel life is not worth living. Try to understand that each successive shock of miscarriage is like a pencil mark on top a previous mark, each one intensifying the other. You will tap into your grief over your previous miscarriage and feel like it has not diminished. You will have an exceedingly difficult time proceeding with the next pregnancy.

Some women, after successive, undiagnosed miscarriages, cannot continue, and they give up their quest for motherhood. Other women work all the harder to find a specialist able to diagnose the reasons for their miscarriages and are determined to continue, no matter how many miscarriages they must endure.

As the shock wears off, you will find putting together an active physical program and educating yourself to your medical choices will help you feel optimistic about your future. Continuing against the odds is difficult; you really must *want* to have children. Remember that most women who have miscarried once or several times do become pregnant and do carry their babies to full term. You and your partner can hope for this too.

Questions to Ask Yourself

1. Do I still feel out of control and anxious? Am I still crying and depressed every day? Am I really ready to try again if I haven't settled my feelings on this loss?
2. Do I think that another pregnancy will replace the baby I just lost? Will having another baby make me feel better, less lost and less lonely?
3. Can I deal with the real prospect of another miscarriage, or does the thought of going through it again seem too much to bear?
4. Can I laugh and do I have moments of happiness and contentment?
5. Do I like my doctor or health care provider, and do I want to go through another pregnancy with her or his help?
6. Do the father and I feel ready to go through another pregnancy as a team, working together for our baby?

Actions to Take

1. Find a grief support group and resolve any feelings of grief before trying to become pregnant again.
2. Set aside special time with the father to discuss your mutual decision about making a family based on your long-term commitment to each other.
3. Before getting pregnant again, discuss with your health care provider what tests you should take to avoid another miscarriage.
4. Don't use pink or patterned toilet paper because they both look like a miscarriage has started when wet with urine.

5. With help, stop smoking and limit your intake of caffeine and alcohol gradually until you can eliminate them from your diet comfortably.
6. When pregnant, join or create a high risk-mothers support group, even if just a phone network.

5

Life
Stories

When your miscarriage is still fresh in your mind, it seems that you are the only one to have endured such a terrible experience. As you share your story, you may hear many similar stories. Gradually, you realize that other couples have had the same crushing disappointment. It is helpful to learn how other women and couples cope with the event and search for solutions, how they adapt and change to meet their goals, taking each day step by step. And you can gain inspiration by reading how couples work through the adversity of miscarriage together to achieve their goals.

Although the names of those I interviewed have been changed, their stories, their feelings, and their lives are all true.

Miscarriage

Miscarriage strikes even those who seem to be the perfect candidates for pregnancy. Young and strong, in good health from a fastidious regime of healthy food and exercise, the body should perform just the way it is supposed to but, even then, miscarriages can occur. The shock when you have worked to achieve perfect health, set up your life to be ready, and then said "go," can burst the bubble of the emotionally strong, reducing the former can-doer into a basket case of tears for months.

Margaret met Chris on a study trip to Europe, and because they were both joggers, she spent time with him apart from the other group members. When they returned to America, they dated for three years before becoming engaged. Once married, they found they had different ideas about the right time to start their family. Margaret was ready right away; Chris wasn't. They agreed to wait five years. During that time Margaret worked in a retail job that was both strenuous and stressful. When she found out she was pregnant, she happily quit her job and settled down to enjoy the process of becoming a mother.

Margaret bought pregnancy books to read because she didn't know what to expect. She enjoyed meeting with her pregnant friends and sharing different physical symptoms and mothering feelings. With every expectation of a normal pregnancy, she continued to jog and swim regularly.

When suddenly she started to spot, she called her doctor immediately. He reassured her that most women spot during pregnancy and she really didn't have a problem. He did recommend that she restrict her exercise. Margaret had promised her sister that she would fly out to baby-sit her nieces in the midwest, and she wondered whether she should go. This was to be her sister and her husband's first vacation since their kids were born, and Margaret hated to disappoint them and upset their plans. Because the doctor was so reassuring, Margaret made the trip.

For her month away, everything seemed fine, but on the day Margaret was to return home, she felt a gush of what turned out to be brownish-colored liquid. She began to worry but told herself that everything would be fine. When she got off the airplane, she was bleeding steadily.

Chris was overjoyed to see her after their month apart, but she could only cry because she knew she was losing the baby. Although he had planned a romantic evening, she only wanted him to hold her while she cried. In the morning she called the doctor, who immediately scheduled her to come in for an ultrasound. She began drinking water for the procedure as the doctor had ordered; consequently she felt bloated and experienced terrible pressure in her bladder on the trip to the specialist's office.

She was physically uncomfortable lying on the ultrasound table. But she was shocked to hear the technician ask whether she was pregnant. In a skeptical tone, the technician asked her when she thought she had become pregnant, questioned whether she had the date wrong, and demanded a catalogue of her symptoms.

Margaret was stunned by the questions. The technician sent her to the bathroom to get ready for a vaginal ultrasound. As she wiped herself, Margaret found a large grayish lump in her hand. When she realized it was a baby, she screamed and cried. The technician and nurse rushed in and took the baby, which had little recognizable limbs, and helped her into the office. When she was dressed, the doctor came in and immediately gave her a big hug. Although he wasn't her regular doctor, his warmth and his caring reassured and supported her immeasurably. He called her doctor, made sure she had a ride home—he even volunteered to have his nurse drive her—and warned her to watch for the placenta.

Margaret's mother, who had brought her, was sitting anxiously in the waiting room. When Margaret explained what had happened, her mother commented, "at least it wasn't a life form yet." Margaret cried harder, her tears from hurt that her mother so misunderstood how she was feeling as well as from grief.

Margaret's husband Chris was distressed about the loss of the baby but inadvertently caused her more pain. That weekend, he was expecting a business client from France who had entertained him in his home while Chris was traveling, and he wanted to reciprocate. Margaret tried to say no, but it seemed so important to Chris that she agreed to put on a dinner for the client and his wife. Chris promised to do his share by cleaning the house and mowing the lawn. Over the weekend, he had an extra load of office work so none of his chores got done. Margaret was left to clean, shop, and cook. Even though she had planned a simple meal, she was exhausted. All her plans to make the dinner easier seemed for naught when Chris spilled ink on the tablecloth. She had to reset the table she had so carefully set the night before.

Because she didn't think she could make conversation with strangers when she still felt so grief-stricken over losing the baby, she invited a good friend and her husband to join them for dinner. When the couple arrived,

Margaret could only stare. How could she have forgotten that her friend was pregnant? When the clients arrived, even though Chris had told them about the miscarriage, the wife began talking about her family and her babies. Finally Margaret escaped to the kitchen and began to cry. Her friend's husband came in, saw her tears, and disappeared to fetch Chris. Chris took her to the bedroom where Margaret cried for thirty minutes before she was finally able to face everyone and carry on with dinner.

When Chris left to drive the guests home, Margaret wanted to take every dirty plate and break it on the floor. After Chris came home and they talked, he understood for the first time what a strain she had been under and the depth of her feelings about the baby's death. He had no idea how she felt and was distressed when he realized he had not paid attention to her or taken time to think about what the baby's death meant to her. In his eagerness to repay his client's hospitality, he had not considered the burden he placed on Margaret when she was too vulnerable and fragile to bear it.

Margaret now feels she learned to stand up for herself because of the incident. The miscarriage helped her and Chris to examine how they communicated with each other, and their discussions have helped them both reconsider their plans for a family. Margaret feels that she and Chris now share an equal level of eagerness and expectation in starting a family.

Margaret went in to see her doctor again to find out what caused the miscarriage. She scheduled a hysterosalpingogram and discovered that she had a uterine septum which the doctor plans to remove. She feels much better knowing the septum probably caused the miscarriage and she is taking her temperature to establish her cycle for the next pregnancy. Margaret is looking forward to being a mother again.

Abortion, Miscarriage, and Trying Again

> *When you are young unplanned things happen just as they do when you are older, but you may have less control of your life and more limited choices. Young women who become pregnant as teenagers may long to have their babies but have abortions because that seems, under the circumstances, to be their only choice. Later in life, when these women are ready to have a family, it seems like a punishment, a payback for the baby given up earlier when a miscarriage occurs. Women in this situation are haunted by the pain of the abortion, and their guilt and self-blame complicates their miscarriage grief.*

Nancy was fifteen, Catholic, and dating a guy who was twenty. When she became pregnant, he was terrified that her parents would have him arrested for statutory rape so threatened to break off their relationship and deny the baby was his. She felt she had no choice but to have a secret abortion. Later, she went on to marry the father, but the marriage did not work, and eventually they divorced.

While she was separated, she went swing dancing at a local bar. There she met Larry, who became a good friend and confidant during her divorce. Eventually, they realized they were in love and began to live together. When Nancy told her ex-husband that she and Larry were moving in together, he cruelly taunted her, "does your boyfriend know you are a baby-killer?"

Larry and Nancy talked about family, and they both wanted children, but felt it necessary to wait until their finances were under control. Both wanted to pay off their bills so Nancy could stay home with the baby.

Eventually, with careful planning, stinting, and lots of hard work, Nancy and Larry put their finances in order. Then several family emergencies occurred, and Larry and Nancy delayed again. Finally, when everything calmed down, Nancy went off the pill.

To her joy, Nancy learned she was pregnant. But at about the same time, her grandmother became ill and was hospitalized. Because of this situation, Nancy didn't see how she could joyfully announce her pregnancy. She went to the hospital and told her grandmother, who was barely conscious. Later, a nurse who had overheard told Nancy's mother, who then told everyone in the family. Nancy felt terrible having everyone know so early in the pregnancy. After her grandmother died, she felt even worse because the family grief overshadowed her pregnancy.

Still, throughout her grieving for her grandmother, Nancy felt physically well, and at the twelve-week mark all seemed to bode well for the pregnancy. In her thirteenth week, her pants felt too tight, so on her way to the doctor's office she stopped at a maternity store and bought a suitcase full of new maternity clothes. In the store, she felt a strange gush from her vagina but didn't worry about it.

At the doctor's office, her regular doctor was gone, and the nurse practitioner couldn't find a heartbeat. She joked with Nancy that it was so late on a Friday afternoon that the baby was napping. She brought in an ultrasound technician, who looked and looked at the screen then got up and went out. When a strange doctor came in, Nancy knew something was wrong. The doctor said he thought her baby was dead, but she would need to have blood work done. After handing her a form, he left the office.

Nancy could hardly get up and put on her clothes. She went to the lab and had blood drawn, then, in a trance, drove home alone in the rush hour traffic. At home, she cried and cried with Larry. She still felt pregnant but knew the doctor was right. The nurse practitioner called her at work on Monday to tell her the baby was dead and to give her the option of having a D & C or waiting for the miscarriage to occur. Nancy put down the phone and began to cry. One of her co-workers, a woman she didn't really know, put her arm around her and offered to take her home. But since Larry worked nearby, he came immediately.

Nancy didn't want to have the D & C because she remembered the abortion. Larry talked to her for a long time and urged her to have it done so she could heal and become pregnant sooner. She had the D & C under local anesthetic and was home soon, crying again.

Back at work, Nancy finds every hour a painful reminder of her loss. Everyone at work seems to be having a baby. One worker who had a miscarriage is now pregnant and pesters Nancy constantly with talk about teddy bear sales and special maternity shops. Nancy can't believe anyone could be so insensitive to not understand that she doesn't want to hear about anything to do with babies. The office has a small staff, and everyone takes coffee breaks and lunch together. Coping with such relationships has strained Nancy to the extent that she feels she is losing control. She hates the job, resents her co-workers' attitudes, but feels trapped by the financial necessity to work.

Larry has been supportive throughout the experience, and they are trying to become pregnant again. At first, Nancy thought she and Larry should have intercourse every day around her ovulation, but her miscarriage group taught her about the ovulation chart and advised her to have sex only every other day. Once her period was late and her hopes were up, but in the middle of the night she felt acute pain, and in the morning passed a liver-like clot. She was so distressed that she didn't go back to the doctor and has stopped tracking her BBT chart.

She still wants to try, but again and again she finds herself thinking that her miscarriage was caused by her abortion. She feels she did something awful and may never become a mother. The earlier baby haunts her, no matter what she tries to think about. The death of her grandmother coming so close to the miscarriage intensifies her grief. The situation at work with her co-workers makes her despondent, but she is not sure she can find another job.

Nancy is in the middle of her grief, and all the complicating factors of her life overwhelm her. She loves her husband and is grateful for his concern, patience, and willingness to wait out the grief, but she wonders how long he will be able to stand it.

The women in the miscarriage group were concerned for Nancy. She cried continually while telling her story. They counseled her to take disability leave and, when she expressed the concern that her boss wouldn't allow it, let her know that she was protected by federal regulations. The leader suggested she call for some one-on-one counseling covered by her HMO to give her the opportunity to talk about her feelings. Her accumulated grief from the abortion, the miscarriage, and the death of her grandmother were more than she could bear.

At times in every person's life, troubles seem to gang up. The saying "trouble comes in threes" testifies to this. The paralyzing symptoms of grief made Nancy feel like a helpless victim without choices, and her work situation made her feel even more powerless. At this point, taking time away from major stresses and seeking extra support may help Nancy focus and process her grief. Nancy has wisely stopped trying to get pregnant to allow time to resolve her emotional state. With the warm and loving help of her husband, and with the support of additional counseling and her miscarriage group, Nancy looks forward to resolving her grief and depression before she goes on to motherhood.

Therapeutic Abortion and Then Two Live Births

The joy of being pregnant comes with a built-in optimism that your child is perfect, and everything about the growth of your baby will go smoothly. It is an exciting moment when you first see your baby moving on ultrasound. But when the health care professional studies the ultrasound or the test results from an amniocentesis too carefully then becomes quiet and suggests you dress and come into the office, you can barely move with fear. When you get the news that your child has severe abnormalities, you think it is more than you can bear. For some mothers, hearing that they must have a therapeutic abortion seems impossible to comprehend. That they must make the decision seems more than anyone can ask. And yet, this is what motherhood is about— a series of decisions over a lifetime in the best interests of the child.

Sally and her husband David were both working, on the go all the time like most couples in their twenties. After some discussion, they decided the time was right to start their family, and Sally went off the birth control pills, not expecting to get pregnant for at least six months. Before she was really ready, she found out she was pregnant and went in for a checkup with her obstetrician, a woman she really liked and trusted. At the first ultrasound she saw the baby's heart beating and everything seemed fine. She was getting over her first feeling that she wasn't quite ready for a baby and getting excited when she went for the second ultrasound.

There were spots on the baby's brain. Sally's doctor sent her to a specialist, who was vague about what the spots meant to the health of the baby. Sally went back to her OB, who suggested Sally have an amnio. The amnio was conclusive: the baby's brain had developed abnormally and Sally would probably miscarry soon. If the baby went to full term, it would die after birth.

Sally was stunned and couldn't seem to make a decision. By now, she was twenty weeks pregnant. Her husband wanted her to make the choice whether to have a therapeutic abortion or wait to miscarry naturally, but Sally changed her mind hour by hour.

She went back to her OB. Her doctor brought her into the office and sat her down. After a long silence, she told Sally gently that she was ready to make the decision, that she had gone to the amnio with the understanding that she would be making a choice. Sally scheduled a therapeutic abortion with a general anesthesia.

Sally hated the outpatient clinic, which was filled with women who couldn't have hurt as much as she did, aching for the loss of her baby. Sally found the therapeutic abortion was not difficult, but the insertion of the laminaria plug to dilate the cervix seemed exceedingly painful. Her doctors and nurses were caring and considerate. The doctor did tell Sally and David their baby was a boy, but did not give them the choice of seeing him.

Sally went home and bled for two days. She had the post-partum hormone blues and cried, slept, and rested. Her family gathered around her with love and support. Her doctor had suggested Sally and David go off for a vacation together after the procedure, and David had arranged a vacation in Hawaii. During her time there, she felt depressed and passive. As things happened around her, she felt like an observer rather than a participant. She couldn't fend off the feeling that the baby's death was her fault, that she hadn't wanted the baby enough, or that the baby would have been healthy if she hadn't gone skiing.

Afterward, Sally's doctor insisted the couple go to counseling. David agreed, but Sally was adamantly opposed. Finally both David and the doctor talked her into it. Together they went for four visits, and Sally found it the best thing she could have done. She is convinced that she recovered from the experience faster.

After some time healing, Sally and David tried again and are now the parents of two healthy children, a boy and a girl. The first baby's death has not been forgotten but is now remembered without the knife-sharp pain of grief.

Miscarriages, Infertility, and Hopes

When you are young, life seems to stretch before you in the limitless luxury of "plenty of time," but many women are surprised to find infertility eating away their finite time of fertility. If you have trouble becoming pregnant and are in your thirties, each month that ticks off the calendar may seem a serious loss, the impending end of fertility looming larger every day. A miscarriage carries the echo of a door slamming.

Mary and her husband Allen had been married happily since their twenties, but they were busy working and learning what being a couple meant. They weren't ready to have a family and never dreamed they might have a problem. All around them, their friends who wanted babies made the decision, and then boom—they were pregnant.

By the time Mary and Allen decided they were ready, she was thirty-one. When month after month of unprotected sex brought no signs of pregnancy, they began to get concerned. They started to become consistent, planning intercourse every month around ovulation time. When Mary still did not get pregnant, they consulted a doctor. About this time they moved so Mary started again with new doctors. They taught her about ovulation charts and wanted her to continue for six months without contraceptives and without fertility intervention. Hearing the months of the calendar rustling by, Mary followed instructions but worried.

At the end of the time period, Mary became a fertility patient and began testing. She soon learned that she wasn't ovulating every month, or if she was, wasn't releasing an egg. Allen's semen analysis showed he had low motility due to a low-grade infection so he was put on antibiotics. In three months, Mary discovered she was on day 36 and hadn't started her period. When her home pregnancy test turned blue, she called her doctor. He ordered her in for a blood test. When the nurse called with the good news, Mary started crying and had to ask her to repeat, "Congratulations, you are pregnant" several times in order to comprehend that at last, it had happened to her. All she could think of was that finally they were going to become parents.

The vaginal ultrasound showed a tiny fetus with a beating heart. Mary and Allen were overjoyed and left clutching the sonogram picture. Although Mary felt fine and both she and Allen were overjoyed, disaster awaited them. Mary went off to the twelve-week checkup alone, feeling happy and confident. Then in one quiet minute, her doctor told her there was no heartbeat—just a sac, larger than before, but no sign of life. Mary described going from happiness and joy to total dismay in one second with the words, "I don't find any heartbeat." She called her husband on her car phone. She cried when she heard his voice and cried more when she got home. Given the choice, she decided to have the D & C, but because it was almost a weekend, she had to wait until the following Tuesday.

That weekend was the longest in her life. She wanted to hibernate, she wanted the world to stand still, and she couldn't stop crying. The worst was that she still felt pregnant, but knew the baby was dead. She began to worry about the D & C because she had never before had surgery and was anxious about having general anesthesia. Worrying about the surgery distracted her from her grief.

She found the surgery the easiest part. Everyone was caring and kind throughout the procedure and she felt no physical pain. But the next morning, her grief and her crashing hormones hit, and she woke up screaming angry that she had lost her baby. In time her body returned to a normal hormonal balance and these feelings passed. She got back into her routine, still stunned that her long awaited pregnancy was over.

Now thirty-five, Mary has gone back on clomid to make sure she releases an egg every month and is waiting to become pregnant again. She and Allen find the scheduled sex to meet the ovulation pattern difficult and less satisfying emotionally. Their quest for a child is changing the quality of their life. The puppy they had gotten just before the miscarriage has been a strong outlet for her nurturing, and Mary gardens, buys herself flowers, and treats herself well to keep happy and in a good frame of mind to become pregnant again. She feels that because she has not become pregnant again, she grieves more for the baby. Mary works to maintain a positive attitude, not say "if" but "when" I have a baby, and she is hopeful that the future will find her and Allen parents.

Mary finds the lack of support from her family and friends one of the most difficult aspects of the experience. The people she cared about couldn't seem to understand why she continued to grieve for the baby and why she wasn't going back to her good job after the baby's death. Her mother-in-law has been particularly insensitive, which has made family gatherings unpleasant for Mary. Now that another relative is newly pregnant, Mary has stopped going to family holidays because she is so uncomfortable. She tries to surround herself with people who make her feel good and ignores those who are uncaring and insensitive to her situation.

Mary went to a miscarriage group after her baby died, then left the group as she felt stronger. Nearing the anniversary of her due date, she returned to the group, finding solace and companionship with the other women. She and Allen planted a tree in their back yard in memory of their little baby. Mary wants more than ever to be a parent and to have a baby, but she is determined not to become financially and emotionally broken from the experience. She says she thinks someday she will be a parent, but she just doesn't know when.

Infertility, Surgeries, a Long Wait, an Anticipated Adoption, and then a Live Birth

Although folk history says if you get ready to adopt, or do adopt, you will become pregnant, statistics don't bear the myth out. Yet here is a family that fought infertility with all the technology of science, to no seeming avail, and then the magic happened. Their daughter will soon be a year old.

Bill and Susan met when Susan was in her twenties and Bill was in his early thirties. Bill was older but loved kids and really wanted a family. Although Susan had a career, she wanted to have a family as well. They lived together for five years before they married. The time seemed right to start a family so Susan stopped taking oral contraceptives. Together they went to see the obstetrician, who suggested they wait about five months and then try to get pregnant. In his excitement Bill went out and bought a tiny pair of baby shoes.

Susan went month after month waiting to find out she was pregnant. Finally her doctor suggested a hystero-salpingogram and discovered that a small ovarian cyst was blocking one fallopian tube. By the time she went in for surgery, the cyst was grapefruit size.

After removal, there was still no pregnancy. Susan and Bill tried clomid and pergonal for three months each, but still nothing happened. Susan had another laparoscopy which revealed that one of her fallopian tubes was blocked. It was subsequently lazered to clear it out. Then in a routine examination, Susan's doctor noticed her thyroid was enlarged and scheduled surgery to remove the thyroid, Susan began taking synthetic thyroid pills daily. Her doctor was confident that the thyroid had been throwing off the hormonal balance, and that now she would become pregnant.

Nothing happened. Susan was still not pregnant despite all the careful timing of sex with her ovulation charts and her attention to keeping herself fit and healthy. Susan and Bill were now up against the time clock because Bill was approaching his fiftieth birthday. They decided that since they wanted kids, they would adopt. They had signed on with an adoption lawyer and had begun writing their stories for the adoption pamphlet when Susan missed a period. Regardless, they had photos taken and were ready to go to print. A pregnancy test brought them the joyful results. Susan was pregnant. She took all the testing because of their ages, but their luck held. The pregnancy was normal and they went on to have a baby girl, one month premature because the amniotic fluid had drained. Although the baby was very little, she was born healthy.

Both Susan and Bill are overjoyed with their baby, and even though the years of medical procedures and charts were hard ones, it all seems worthwhile to them.

Miscarriages and then Adoption

Although we all like stories with "happy ever after" endings, we know that they are relatively rare. When a couple appears to have an idyllic life, family and friends may worry because it seems too good to be true. When Henry and Barbara met, all their friends were overjoyed that two such kind and generous people had fallen in love and wanted to start a family. And then their troubles began. . . .

Henry and Barbara met later in life. Introduced by a mutual friend, Henry was in his late thirties and Barbara was in her forties. After a year of dating, Henry proposed to Barbara; she accepted with joy. Barbara recalled a night on the beach when she and Henry realized they had both traveled and experienced many different things, but now both wanted to settle down and have a family.

They were married in Gibraltar and honeymooned in Seville. They stayed in an old hotel filled with antiques. In their room was a cradle, which both of them felt was a kind of magical sign. Indeed, Barbara became pregnant on the honeymoon, and they were both thrilled they were to be parents.

When Barbara went in to her first appointment, the nurse practitioner was unable to hear any sound with the Doppler. The nurse wasn't concerned because she said it might be too early; at the next appointment, she assured Barbara, they would certainly hear the heartbeat. Before the next appointment, Barbara, because of her age was going to have chorionic villus sampling done for chromosomal abnormalities and for sex determination. Just before she left for the regional hospital to be tested, she noticed spotting. She called her doctor, but he seemed unalarmed and suggested she carry on with her plans for testing.

Barbara describes lying on the table while the technician worked the sonogram and suddenly realizing she was taking too long to locate the baby. When the technician left the room and the physician returned, she knew there was a problem. The doctor told her he thought she was going to have a miscarriage. Barbara decided not to have a D & C, instead choosing to go home and let the miscarriage happen naturally. After several days, she had cramping and passed a liver-like clot of tissue.

Still determined, Barbara and Henry waited two to three months before trying again. After six months with no success, Barbara and Henry went to a fertility expert for additional help. With clomid, Barbara became pregnant but began spotting and again miscarried at eight weeks. This time there was light cramping, but she never saw any tissue. Consulting with another fertility specialist, Barbara got a diagnosis that she was not producing eggs. Although she privately disagreed with the diagnosis, Barbara found that a workmate she knew had donated eggs before, and she approached her to become a donor for herself and Henry. She became pregnant again, but miscarried even earlier than before.

Now her doctors thought she was producing a suboptimal endometrium, which meant that the lining of her uterus was insufficient to support a fertilized egg. Taking progesterone did not seem to make an appreciable difference. At this point, Henry said he thought they should forget the treatments and try adoption. He was concerned that the escalating use of the drugs would have a long-term physical affect on Barbara.

Henry is puzzled at the social attitude of shame about adoption. He feels strongly that there should be no embarrassment. If a couple is unable to conceive or to carry a baby full term, then adoption is a reasonable choice for two people who love each other and want a family. If they are able to provide for children, to love children, to raise children, what difference does it make whether the child is born to them or adopted by them?

The adoption process took Barbara and Henry three years, which they both think was longer than normal. Most couples are able to adopt a baby within six months to a year. In their case, it took a while to find a baby. One birth mother wanted to share custody of the child, another couple arrived complete with tattoos and a jail record. Then they made a painful discovery that another birth mother was accepting expense money from two other couples.

Finally, a random call came to their lawyer from a young pregnant woman in the midwest who already had one eighteen-month old and she knew she wouldn't be able to take care of another child. She wanted a placement far away from her home. They talked to her on the phone, and then, with both excitement and anxiety, flew to her hometown to meet her. They found her mother supportive and helpful, and she herself seemed determined to give the baby up for adoption.

After the months passed, Barbara flew to the city to be there when the baby was born. As labor started, Barbara called Henry who caught a flight so all three could be present for the baby's birth. After a week caring for the baby in their motel room, the new family of three flew home.

With much forethought, they decided on open adoption, meaning they would keep in touch with the baby's grandmother, and the baby would always know about her parentage. They think the baby stands a better chance of growing up with a good feeling about her birth mother and her adoptive parents, and they want her to know her grandmother throughout her childhood.

Needless to say, Barbara and Henry are thrilled to be parents at last. Neither one feels like a failure. In fact, they laugh that it was all worth it to get to the point that they can hold their baby in their arms. Their advice is to learn how to manage your emotions and not to invest in too high hopes until you have a sense of how things are going to work out. They both say the most important step is committing to your own goals, and then doing everything possible to meet them. They wanted a baby, and now they have one.

In Summary

The important threads that weave through all of these stories are the tears, pain, and disappointment. Miscarriage brings shock, grief, and sadness. These couples have had to go on with their lives, readjusting to discover new paths to their goals, giving each other love and support, and learning how to share the grief as well as the joy. We never know what will happen to us—happy surprises or dismaying loss seem tossed our way in random fashion. Many women feel that one or two years after the miscarriage, when they finally hold a baby in their arms, all the racking disappointments suddenly seem like nothing at all. For those who still wait for their baby, time seems to stretch out in endless emptiness and frustration. Couples who have chosen childlessness gradually deal with what may be a bitter choice, finding solace in being available for young relatives or neighbors, while enjoying the freedom of childlessness and the continued undiluted intimacy of their relationship.

Making peace with your choices, finding love from your partner, and looking forward to whatever life brings, one day at a time, is all any of us can do to clear our hearts and face the future.

6

What Is Miscarriage?

A miscarriage is the death of your baby
A miscarriage is shattered shards of your
  mothering dream
A miscarriage is physical pain and gushing blood
A miscarriage is returning from the hospital alone
A miscarriage is a nursery without a baby

If you have had a miscarriage, you are suffering deeply distressing feelings of sadness and loss because your baby died. Anyone who loses a baby experiences a sense that the world has been turned upside down. You are shocked, numb with grief, and heartsore.

No matter how far along you were in your pregnancy, if your pregnancy does not result in a baby who becomes part of your family, as you had every right to expect, you must acknowledge your loss to heal yourself. Even if the future seems bleak to you right now, you will gradually recover, but no one can say how soon or how easily. No one can tell you that you ought to feel fine because one week, month, or year has gone by. You will heal in your own time, but accepting your pain will speed your recovery.

You have already read about the grieving process with guideposts to help you through the experience of grief. Now you need to learn exactly what happened to you in your miscarriage. Dispelling some of the myths or simple unknowns will decrease your anxiety and fear about the experience. You may never know what caused your miscarriage, but if you understand the physical process, you can sort out your inevitable but needless feelings of failure and guilt. Knowing the physical consequences of your body's return from pregnancy helps you be patient and accepting of your own recovery process. Once informed about miscarriage, you can make educated choices about bearing a child in the future and becoming a mother at last.

What Is a Miscarriage?

A miscarriage, medically referred to as spontaneous abortion, can happen at any time during pregnancy. A miscarriage occurs when the fetus is expelled from the uterus, dying before or during the expulsion. There may be blood (different amounts for each woman), cramping—from minimal to severe—and depending on the length of the pregnancy, tissue, liver-like blood clots, or a fetus with discernible features. The miscarriage can happen suddenly without warning, or take a week or more of spotting and bleeding to finish. Sometimes not all the tissue is expelled, and medical intervention is called for to avoid infections from material remaining in the uterus.

A number of different types of miscarriages can occur. Some of them happen in the first trimester, others in the second or third trimester. Most of the early miscarriages occur between the seventh week and the sixteenth week. Late miscarriages, called stillbirths, occur between the seventeenth and the twenty-eighth week. As the baby develops, the reasons for the miscarriage change, although some of the same problems may occur in the first and second trimesters. Because the causes are different, treatments for prevention may differ.

A Threatened Miscarriage

When you begin spotting and bleeding, even if it just looks like a brownish stain, your health care provider may recommend you go to bed and abstain from sexual intercourse. It is not clear medically whether such intervention has any affect on the miscarriage, but you will feel that you are doing everything you can to save your baby. Spotting after intercourse can occur because the cervix is tender and will bleed slightly, but this is different from a threatened miscarriage if it occurs only after intercourse. Spotting may also occur around the time you would have your period if you were not pregnant.

Report any spotting to your medical health provider immediately. Start a record of all your symptoms, including the day they started, what you were doing when they started, and whether they are accompanied by menstrual-type cramping and lower back pain.

An Early Miscarriage (Spontaneous Abortion)

The most common miscarriage is the death of a baby as she or he grows in the uterus, occurring in the first sixteen weeks of pregnancy. Termed medically a "spontaneous abortion," this miscarriage is signaled by spotting, which gradually increases to a gush of bright red blood mixed with clots of tissue. The spotting may start and then stop, and even a week later start again. The amount of bleeding accompanying the miscarriage is different for each woman. The fetus is expelled through the cervix and the vagina, sometimes with the kind of cramping and discomfort you have with your period, sometimes with severe pain.

There are a number of variations to a spontaneous abortion, and you may find your symptoms differ. Generally, the health care community defines miscarriage in the following terms:

A threatened abortion: The cervix is still closed but you may have bleeding, spotting, or cramping. You may need a blood test to see whether your hormone levels are adequate to maintain the pregnancy.

An inevitable abortion: The bleeding and cramping increase and you know you are losing your baby. Be sure to contact your doctor and collect all the miscarriage products so you can try to determine the cause of the miscarriage.

A missed abortion: You may not be aware anything has happened to the baby until your health care professional can't find the baby's heartbeat. Ultrasound may show an empty sac. You may still feel pregnant but the baby has died. You may need a D & C to complete the miscarriage and let your body heal.

An incomplete abortion: You body only passed part of the fetal tissue, and you need a D & C to prevent infection and let your body heal.

A *complete abortion:* Your body flushed out all the miscarriage products, and unless you develop an infection or continue bleeding, you probably will need no further medical treatment.

There are a number of causes for spontaneous abortion, which are discussed later in the chapter, but the majority of early miscarriages occur because the fertilized egg or the fetus carries a genetic abnormality stemming from the sperm, the egg, or the combining of chromosomes in the growing fertilized egg that becomes the fetus.

Use a clean plastic bag to collect all the miscarriage material. If the miscarriage goes into the toilet bowl, use a kitchen sieve to collect all the tissue you can. Call your health care provider immediately, and follow her or his instructions about where to take the tissue for a chromosomal examination. Although expensive, this will give you an opportunity to see if chromosomal irregularities caused the death of the baby.

Care for Recovery

If your health care provider feels the miscarriage has been completely expelled, she or he will send you home with the proviso that you check back if there is any further bleeding, cramping, or if you begin to run a temperature, which signals an infection is starting from tissue remaining in the uterus.

If they suspect you may have an incomplete abortion, meaning some of the fetal tissue remained in the uterus, a D & C will be scheduled. This out-patient medical procedure may be done under a local anesthetic to the cervix, or if you and your health care professional choose, general anesthesia. To cleanse the fetal tissue from the uterus, the health care provider uses a medical tool that gently removes all fetal tissue and the endometrium, or uterine lining, from the uterus.

After your D & C you may go home. Rest until you feel able to resume your daily schedule. Be sure to drink plenty of liquids, at least two quarts of water, milk, or juice a day. Eat normal amounts of well-balanced meals and try to avoid either binging or not eating at all. Expect to have post-miscarriage blues from hormonal readjustment as your body returns to its pre-pregnancy state.

Schedule a visit with your health care provider in two weeks even if none has been suggested. Abstain from oral or vaginal sex until after your checkup to allow the uterus to heal without risk of infection.

Ectopic (Tubal) Pregnancy

Sometimes the fertilized egg implants and begins to grow outside the uterus. It may burrow into the abdomen wall, the ovary, or one of the fallopian tubes. Called an ectopic pregnancy, it is doomed to failure. Very intense abdominal or shoulder pain may signal an ectopic pregnancy and an ultrasound will confirm the unusual location of the pregnancy. If you have any of these symptoms, check with your doctor immediately because an ectopic pregnancy can be life-threatening and can affect your future fertility.

Usually an ectopic pregnancy lodges in one of the fallopian tubes. Your eggs are released from the ovary and travel through the fallopian tube every month, usually alternating tubes. The sperm meet the egg in the fallopian tube. Sometimes a fertilized egg will implant in the tube instead of traveling to the uterus to implant. The fallopian tube is a location too narrow and small for the growing fetus.

A miscarriage may spontaneously occur or else a doctor must perform surgery by laparoscope and laser to remove the pregnancy and save the mother's life. If not removed, the fetus will rupture the fallopian tube and set off internal hemorrhaging, which can be life-threatening. When discovered early enough, surgery can be scheduled to prevent the pregnancy from permanently damaging one of the tubes, consequently decreasing fertility for future pregnancies. There is no way to transplant an ectopic pregnancy from the abnormal location into the uterus.

An ectopic pregnancy may be discovered when you test pregnant but there is no indication of change in your uterus. Usually intense pain signals this very serious problem. If your provider discovers the problem while you are at your regular checkup or even when you come in as an emergency due to the pain, she or he may require that you go immediately into surgery. This can be terrifying, both facing the surgery and the shock of realizing you will be losing your baby shortly. Sadly, you have absolutely no choice. You face the possibility of dying without the removal of the pregnancy.

Under general anesthesia, your doctor will make a small incision along your pubic hairline. She or he will insert a laparoscope and, with care, make a further incision into the fallopian tube itself. Using the laparoscope, all the fetal tissue is removed and sutures applied to close the inner incisions with stitches on the exterior incision. You will remain in the hospital after the surgery for at least three to six days.

If you have had a medical emergency, both your doctor and the father will be happy to have saved your life and perhaps to have saved your fallopian tube from rupturing, important for your future fertility. Still, in the midst of their jubilation, they may not remember that you have had a pregnancy loss, and that the procedure meant the end of this pregnancy and your hopes for this child.

Women in this situation are often in conflict, mentioning the death of the baby instead of their gratitude for being alive and their appreciation for their surgeon's skill. If you experienced this tragedy, remember that you can feel both the grief at your loss and the joy at being alive simultaneously. The abruptness and seriousness of the surgery and the grief over the death of your baby make the experience a difficult one for women to assimilate.

Care for Recovery

Because you have had major surgery, you will be tender and sore for three or more weeks and may require as much as six weeks to return to feeling physically well. Rest in bed for three to four days after you return home, or until you feel able to resume a limited physical schedule.

Even as you begin to return to your daily routine, set aside a regular time for a daily rest and avoid tiring throngs of visitors, excursions, parties, or other events. Especially when you are tired, you will find yourself on an emotional roller coaster. Keep reminding yourself that besides grieving for your baby, you must deal with the aftermath of your medical emergency and subsequent surgery. Expect to have post-miscarriage blues from hormonal readjustment as well as post-surgery letdown.

Follow the usual diet recommendations: drink plenty of liquids, eat well-balanced meals, and avoid alcoholic beverages (they may increase your depression).

Again, schedule a visit with your health care provider in two weeks. Abstain from oral or vaginal sex until after your checkup to allow the uterus to heal without risk of infection.

Intrauterine Fetal Death

After sixteen weeks, the death of a baby while in the uterus is called an intrauterine fetal death. If it occurs before fetal movement is noticed, the death is often found during a routine appointment viewing on a sonogram or by listening to the baby on ultrasound. The health care provider will not be able to locate a heartbeat. Later in the pregnancy, the mother usually has the intuition that something is wrong, sometimes because the baby stops kicking or moving. Sometimes she has no idea anything unusual has occurred, and during a regularly scheduled appointment, the health care provider cannot find a heartbeat. An ultrasound may show that the fetus is not functioning normally or is no longer present.

When an intrauterine death occurs, the parents face difficult choices. Labor can be induced immediately by drugs, or the mother can wait for the body's normal processes to start labor naturally, causing the baby to be delivered.

Some women want time with their baby still in the uterus, and they prefer to wait for the spontaneous onset of delivery. Other women want the baby delivered immediately. There is no right or wrong way to deal with an intrauterine fetal death; the way the parents choose is usually best. The delivery of a stillborn can be both a relief and a devastating end of the parents' dream for a baby.

If you deliver late in your pregnancy, you may need medical care to help you with breast engorgement. Your body was ready for nursing; consequently, even though you lost your baby, your breasts can become painfully hard and swollen with milk after delivery. This can be a very difficult reminder of what you lost when your baby died, especially when you are home alone. Your doctor can prescribe medication, and cold compresses will also help reduce the pain.

Care for Recovery

If you have had a stillbirth delivery, you will need a great deal of time to recover from the physical and emotional trauma of the delivery and to return your body to pre-pregnancy condition. You will be tender and sore for three or more weeks. Stay in bed for at least three to four days after you return home, and don't be afraid to extend this time if you don't feel recovered. Remember, your body needs plenty of rest to recover and heal. Starting your schedule before you can physically take the strain can set you back and delay your recovery.

Avoid tiring throngs of visitors, excursions, parties, or other events. Don't forget that being around people is tiring, and when you are tired, emotions can overwhelm you. Ask your partner to help you screen out visitors so you see only people you really want to see and who will comfort you.

Therapeutic Abortion

The complexity of the growth and development of a baby means a number of serious problems can develop throughout the pregnancy. If testing, usually by amniocentesis, shows abnormalities in development or permanent disabilities, the parents may choose a therapeutic abortion.

If you are forced to make the decision to end your pregnancy in the best interests of your baby, your grief can be overwhelming. This may be the first time you have faced what counselors call a "life decision," and the enormity may feel too heavy for you to bear. You may still feel conflict over your choice, but keep in mind that you have made the best decision you could; life decisions are always searingly painful. Even when you are confident you made the right decision, you will feel deeply grieved, sad, and angry that you were forced into the tragic situation.

Care for Recovery

You have had major surgery and you will be tender and sore for three or more weeks. Your body will take time to recover, and you must give it that time.

Even as you begin to return to your daily routine, set aside a regular time for a rest and avoid getting over-tired. Expect to have post-miscarriage blues from hormonal readjustment as well as post-surgery letdown.

Follow the usual diet recommendations: drink plenty of liquids, eat well-balanced meals, and avoid alcoholic beverages (they may increase your depression).

Schedule a visit with your health care provider in two weeks. Abstain from oral or vaginal sex until after your checkup to allow the uterus to heal without risk of infection.

The Known Reasons for Miscarriage

The growth and development of a fetus from a few cells to a full-term baby involves intricate chemical balances and an enormous number of molecular divisions that result in tissue growth. At every step, there is the possibility that something will go wrong. Scientists do not completely understand the delicate communication between the mother's body and the developing fetus, but somehow abnormalities send a signal, probably chemical, and the mother's body rejects the fetus and a miscarriage occurs.

There are a number of potential problems besides chromosomal abnormalities. Sometimes miscarriages occur because of cervical, uterine, or placental problems that create an environment unable to sustain the healthy fetus, thus leading to its consequent death. For example, the cervix, ordinarily a very tough muscle, may have been damaged from previous medical procedures. Later in the pregnancy, it may not be able to hold the weight of the baby. It dilates and effaces under the pressure of the baby and the amniotic sack after the twelfth week of pregnancy, causing miscarriage of a baby before it can survive out of the womb.

Here are some of the specific causes of a miscarriage. Please remember that even though the medical profession knows why some miscarriages occur, your health care provider may never be able to pin down the specific reason yours happened.

Chromosomal Abnormality

Both the chromosomes in the father's sperm and the chromosomes in the mother's egg are responsible for the genetic material which "builds" a baby. Each parent contributes half of the genetic material. Genes are chemicals in the nucleus of every cell, and they carry all the bits of information that govern a body's growth and physical responses. They are carried on long strands of chromosomes, with 46 chromosomes in each normal human cell. These chromosomes link up to be 23 pairs. Any one of the genes can be defective, creating a chromosomal irregularity that can produce abnormal growth in a fetus as well as problems throughout the life of the child.

When a gene is defective, the baby can develop abnormal physical problems in the uterus that can be life-threatening. Early in the pregnancy, the "blighted ovum," which is an egg that develops abnormally, will be rejected and flushed out by the mother's body. Sometimes the genetic defects come from the parents' genes; sometimes they occur while the fetus is developing, causing an interuterine fetal death later in the pregnancy. The older the parents, the greater the chance of chromosomal abnormality.

External environmental elements can cause abnormal chromosomal development, but the inventory of suspects grows and changes every year so there is no definitive listing. Certain drugs, alcohol, tobacco, narcotics, plastics, petroleum products, radiation, and many environmental situations, such as exposure to the light emitted from computer screens, are potential culprits. If you are having miscarriages with no discernible cause, ask your health care provider about exposure to environmental elements.

If you have a miscarriage without any discernible reason, you may want to consult with a genetic counselor for genetic testing. With blood samples, the counselor can determine whether you or the father has hereditary diseases or chromosomal abnormalities that will cause disabling defects in your children. The news may mean you cannot have children using his sperm or your egg.

This can be an overwhelmingly difficult and painful discovery, making the parent with the chromosomal irregularity feel defective, rejected, and defeated. Because there is absolutely nothing the parent can do to change the situation, she or he may become very angry, which can put a great deal of stress on the marital relationship. If you or your partner has an inherited gene problem, you both need to find out what your choices are in the situation and learn what the statistical chances are to have a normal, healthy baby. Try not to dwell on the problem; use your energy to find a solution.

There are still options for couples wanting children when one partner has a hereditary genetic problem. Egg or sperm donors can be considered. You may think of adopting or remaining childless. You will need to take some time to consider your choices and come to a mutual agreement with your partner.

Amniocentesis to Determine Fetal Abnormalities: Amniocentesis determines if a fetus has abnormalities. The process is administered in the fourth month of pregnancy and is recommended for women over 35 years old, women who have a history of spontaneous abortions, and women who have delivered a live baby with abnormalities. The procedure entails inserting a needle under local anesthesia through the abdomen into the uterus. Guided by an ultrasound picture to avoid contact with the fetus, the doctor withdraws a small amount of amniotic fluid. The fetus sheds cells into the fluid, and a researcher can replicate the genetic makeup of the fetus from these cells. With this test, you will know whether your baby has genetic abnormalities that can seriously hinder her or his development.

Although amniocentesis is a routine medical screening procedure, there is a two to five percent risk of having a spontaneous abortion or injuring the fetus in some way, and you need to understand these dangers when deciding to have—or not to have—this procedure. It will be three to four weeks before you get the results, and although the wait is difficult, many women feel knowing their baby is normal is worth it.

If your baby has chromosomal abnormalities, the news will be difficult to accept. If the results report bad news, you will feel numbed and shocked. Take some time to decide with the father and your health care provider whether or not you wish to have the pregnancy terminated by a therapeutic abortion.

Fetal Autopsy: Particularly helpful in diagnosing problems is tissue from a miscarriage which can be genetically tested for abnormalities. Supplying tissue may not always provide answers, but it can rule out some problems. Although it may be upsetting for you to gather tissue, it may be very helpful. If you have experienced your first miscarriage, you may not have known to collect fetal tissue, but if you have more than one, you need to discuss with your health care provider the procedure for collecting a sample. You will need to request a chromosomal workup from the tissue or an autopsy.

Hormonal Imbalance

A very delicate chemical balance is responsible for the timing of releasing your egg and building up the endometrium, the uterine lining, for the fertilized egg to implant in your uterus. Maintaining a hospitable environment in the uterus for the egg and supplying all its needs also requires an ongoing hormonal balance.

Usually, the hormone in question is progesterone, first produced by the corpus luteum after the egg is fertilized, and then by the placenta. Progesterone keeps the uterus from contracting. Spotting and bleeding can be an indication that your level of progesterone is too low to maintain the pregnancy. When there is too little progesterone, miscarriages can occur. A blood test can determine your progesterone level, but the amount each woman needs varies, making it difficult to judge whether the level is sufficient. You can suspect a hormonal imbalance if you have a previous history of menstrual irregularity, infertility, early miscarriages, and continual cramping and spotting early in your pregnancy.

Early forms of synthetic progesterone or DES created genital abnormalities in the daughters of women who took the drug. The current recommended progesterone, hydroxyprogesterone caproate, is derived naturally, and the chemical compound is similar to the compound produced by a woman's body. A number of studies are out concerning the risks of taking progesterone early in the pregnancy to avoid miscarriage, so discuss the situation with your health care provider. Most medical practitioners feel the natural progesterone can be helpful and prescribe it without worry of birth defects.

Polycystic Ovarian Disease: When the hormonal imbalance disturbs normal ovulation patterns, small cysts sometimes form on the ovaries and ovulation does not occur. Women with a history of irregular periods, facial hair, and obesity may want to request a test to find out whether they are suffering hormonal imbalances. Although surgery used to be recommended, it no longer is. Clomiphene may be prescribed to bring the hormones back to their proper levels. Polycystic Ovarian Disease is sometimes called Stein-Leventhal syndrome.

Molar Pregnancy

In this quite rare condition, the placenta forms cysts which interfere with the delivery of nutrients to the fetus and result in its death. There is nothing that can be done to treat this condition. Spontaneous abortion is the normal conclusion.

Illness

When you are not pregnant, normal illness is no cause for alarm, but when pregnant, you should report even a fever to your health care provider. Some illnesses can have a very detrimental effect on your baby. Following are a few conditions that can be particularly harmful to a developing fetus.

Toxoplasmosis: This disease is carried by free-ranging cats who pick up a parasite from rats and mice and pass it through feces. If you have cats, make sure another family member cleans out the cat box, and report all fevers and flu-like symptoms to your doctor.

Rubella: Health professionals thought they had conquered Rubella, or German measles, but there has been a recent resurgence of this disease. If you contract rubella when pregnant in the first trimester, your baby may be born with birth defects or mental retardation. Check with your doctor for a blood test to see if you are immune before you become pregnant again. If you do not have the immunity, you can be vaccinated, but this must be done at least sixty days *before* your next pregnancy.

Pelvic Inflammatory Diseases

A number of vaginal infections can affect fertility and cause fetal injury and death. Some of these diseases have symptoms you can recognize, but some rage silently. You may have had such a low-grade infection in the past without even knowing it. During your pregnancy, you need to pay attention to any change in your vaginal discharge because that may signal a vaginal infection which can affect your baby. Bring any increase or color change of vaginal discharge or itching to the attention of your health care provider.

Chlamydia: This is one of the most common sexually transmitted diseases, but aside from a yellowish discharge and minimal bleeding after intercourse, you may never know you have it. If you have the slightest suspicion you might have this disease, ask your health care provider for a test because chlamydia can be responsible for fetal death and miscarriage.

Gonorrhea: This curable disease has silent symptoms but can cause premature birth or blindness of the baby after a successful delivery. Gonorrhea, unchecked and untreated, damages the fallopian tubes and the ovaries, causing infertility problems. The only symptoms are a slightly irritating vaginal discharge and some irritation when urinating.

Mycoplasmosis: The medical community knows very little about this disease, except that it can rupture the membranes around the fetus and cause miscarriage. There are no symptoms except multiple, unexplained miscarriages; but once the condition is detected, it can be cured with antibiotics.

AIDS: Acquired immune deficiency syndrome can be transmitted by a mother to her unborn child through blood transference or through nursing her baby. This disease can be detected but it cannot be cured. If you have had a blood transfusion or if you have had sex with someone who has AIDS, notify your doctor.

Syphilis: Although not as widespread as it used to be, syphilis is a dangerous disease with a fifty percent fetal death rate. Symptoms come in three stages, the first being sores in the genital area which are replaced by a rash anywhere on the body, sometimes accompanied by runny eyes and sore throat. In the last stage, the heart, brain, and eyes become affected. The baby of a pregnant woman with syphilis, if delivered alive, will have the disease. If you have the slightest suspicion you may have been exposed to this disease, you should be tested for syphilis on your first prenatal visit.

Cytomegalovirus (CMV): Although CMV is a rare virus, its ability to cross the placenta and injure or kill the fetus makes it a very important one to keep track of.

Herpes Virus 2: Herpes is a common sexually transmitted disease with patterns of flare-up and quiescent stages. Initially herpes exhibits symptoms consisting of small sores in the genital area or the mouth, sometimes accompanied by symptoms of the flu. After these apparent symptoms, the virus can remain dormant for many years. Although the virus does not cross the placenta, a vaginal delivery when the virus is present can cause the death of the delivered baby. If you have ever had herpes, you must let your doctor know so she or he can test you at the time of delivery. If your herpes is active, your baby must be delivered by a cesarean section to save its life.

Toxemia

Sudden swelling of your hands or feet after the twenty-fourth week can indicate you have developed toxemia, or preeclampsia. A change in your blood pressure can signal the initial stages of kidney breakdown. Preeclampsia leads to eclampsia with subsequent shutdown of all the major organs, necessitating immediate delivery of the baby to save the life of the mother. Toxemia occurs most often in first pregnancies. If you have been diagnosed with toxemia, you must be carefully monitored in your current pregnancy and any subsequent pregnancies.

Hypertension

Women with high blood pressure must work closely with their health care provider for good preconception care because the pregnancy will put added strain on the

woman's body. Some of the medications given for hypertension are harmful to the fetus, but there are substitute
medicines which are very effective and harmless.
Maintaining a good healthy prenatal program assures
normal fetal growth. High blood pressure can cause insufficient blood circulation to both the uterus and the
placenta so the fetus does not get the nutrition necessary
for normal development. You can learn how to take your
own blood pressure and monitor your condition
carefully.

Diabetes

Diabetes can cause a variety of problems with the fetus
that endanger both baby and mother. Women who had
diabetes before pregnancy or women who develop gesta-
tional diabetes as a result of their pregnancy hormones
are particularly at risk for miscarriage and stillbirth.
Diabetes can be managed through diet and through in-
jections of insulin so most diabetics can still deliver
healthy babies. You will need to take a very active role in
monitoring your condition and working with your health
care professional to keep your blood chemistry at normal
levels.

DES

Diethylstilbestrol was a synthetic hormone similar to estrogen given to pregnant women between 1941 and 1971
as a preventive for miscarriage. In a sad irony, the daughters of those women are themselves more susceptible to

miscarriage because their mothers used the drug. For some women, DES caused abnormalities in their reproductive organs. They may have problems with an incompetent cervix or their fallopian tubes and uterus may be misshapen, which may affect their fertility and their ability to carry a baby full term.

Find out if your mother ever took the drug, and if she did, advise your doctor. With care and close medical supervision, you may be able to avoid miscarriage or premature labor. Women whose mothers took DES are at risk for clear-cell cancers of the vagina or cervix.

RH Factor

The Rh factor (Rh-negative) can be a reason for miscarriage. If you and your baby have a different Rh factor, your body may reject the baby by producing antibodies which will cross the placenta and attack the fetus' red blood cells. In some cases, this causes severe anemia; in others, this incompatibility leads to miscarriage or stillbirth.

Your blood group was inherited, and along with your blood type (A, B, AB, or O) you inherit either a Rh-negative or Rh-positive factor as part of your blood typing. The Rh refers to a protein found on the red blood cells. The more common type, found in 85 percent of all people, is Rh-positive. Those without the protein are called Rh-negative. A blood test will tell you your blood type.

This condition is not severe with first pregnancies, but it increases with each subsequent conception. An amniocentesis test will determine whether your baby has an Rh factor different from yours. If this situation does exist, your health provider will give you shots of Rh immune globulin to prevent your body from producing the antibodies harmful to the fetus. These shots usually begin at 28 weeks.

If you have an incompatibility, your health care provider needs to administer shots to you after any miscarriage, amniocentesis procedure, or abortion to reduce the risk of this problem in subsequent pregnancies. If you develop the antibodies, your health care professional must monitor the fetus carefully. If the fetus develops problems, an early delivery or, in the most life-threatening cases, a complete blood transfusion while the baby is still in the uterus may be necessary.

A-B-O Incompatibility

A baby can inherit the blood type of either the mother or father. If the baby has the father's type, an incompatibility may develop. Normally, a mother's body issues a block to keep the immune system from reacting, but in some cases this block is not issued and the baby is rejected.

Placental Problems

The placenta plays an essential role in delivering nutrients and oxygen to the developing fetus. The placenta develops early in the pregnancy and is delivered as an afterbirth following the baby's delivery. When there is a problem with the placenta, the life of the fetus may be threatened.

The placenta, embedded in the uterine wall, is joined to the baby by the umbilical cord which is like a straw divided into two parts. One side delivers food and oxygen to the baby, and the other is an exit for fetal waste and carbon monoxide. The placenta also produces hormones to regulate the pregnancy; without them, the fetus will die.

Placenta Previa: Normally, a fertilized egg implants itself high up in the uterus, near the exit of the fallopian tube. In some cases the egg drops down and implants near the cervix. Consequently, as the placenta grows, it can expand to cover the cervix, blocking the exit passageway for the mature baby, or creating an unstable attachment that leads to less effective functioning of the placenta. In some cases, the placenta seems to move away from the cervix as the fetus grows, but ordinarily it remains. Whether it totally or partially covers, the fact that it straddles the cervix puts the placenta in hazard of separating or thinning and tearing.

Placenta previa can be indicated by spotting and then bleeding without cramps or pain. The problem can lead to internal hemorrhaging for the mother and to death for the baby. An ultrasound can confirm the diagnosis of placental previa.

A number of treatment possibilities can bring a pregnancy to full term despite this condition. Some medical professionals suggest tying off the cervix (see incompetent cervix) to protect and support the placenta. Medication to prevent uterine labor and contractions and bed rest are also standard treatments. This is a serious medical situation and needs close supervision and attention.

Abruptio Placenta, or Placental Separation: Sometimes the placenta begins to deteriorate and separate from the uterine wall. Depending on the amount of separation and the stage of the pregnancy, this condition can lead to premature delivery or miscarriage, and can threaten the life of the mother. If there is only partial separation, you may be able to continue the pregnancy through the use of medicine and bed rest to stop the hemorrhaging. Your health care provider may order amniocentesis to make sure the baby is not impaired by the condition and has lungs sufficiently developed to survive after delivery.

Searing pain and bleeding can indicate the placenta breaking away from the uterine wall. A sudden drop in blood pressure accompanying the pain and bleeding may indicate complete separation, a serious emergency condition needing immediate medical attention to save the life of the mother and the child.

Malfunctioning Placenta: The medical profession is not clear why, in some cases, the placenta does not perform adequately to support the life of the fetus. A malfunctioning placenta can be caused by blood clots, by infections which weaken the placenta, or by a condition called preeclampsia in the mother. If you notice that your baby has markedly changed her or his activity, contact your doctor immediately. Although there are a number of other possibilities, a fetus that appears normal but is undersized may not be getting the nourishment needed for normal growth and development because the impaired placenta is not delivering the necessary nutrients.

Uterine Abnormalities

The uterus is the womb, or home, for the growing fetus until it is delivered into the outside world. Normally, the fertilized egg implants on the uterine wall about ten days after it has been fertilized by a sperm in the fallopian tube. Once implanted, the egg continues to develop, growing the placenta and the connecting umbilical cord. The body signals a successful implantation and development, and the uterus becomes a closely regulated environment for the fetus. A normal uterus has no problem accepting the growth of the fetus to full term.

In some cases, the uterus is unable to accept the growth of the fetus. Some conditions can be treated by surgery, some cannot; but abnormalities can cause the uterus to signal birth, whether the baby is full term or not.

If you have had a number of undiagnosed miscarriages and have had a problem with urinary tract infections, you need to ask your doctor for a hysterosalpingogram, or X-ray that traces dyes introduced into the uterus.

Uterine Fibroids: Fibroids (myomas) are benign muscle growths that can occur in the uterus. They cause problems when they interfere with implantation, preventing the egg from attaching securely to the uterine wall with the eventual outcome of miscarriage. If the egg does manage to attach itself between the fibroids, the additional hormones released in the uterus to regulate the pregnancy can stimulate growth of the fibroids, leaving little room for the baby. The baby can become malformed, or the crowded condition can signal premature labor.

Removal of fibroids requires major surgery with a five- to six-week recovery time. This surgery must be done before pregnancy.

Misshapen Uterus: Women of mothers who took DES when pregnant may have a misshapen uterus or the condition may occur as a genetic abnormality. Any unusual shape makes it difficult for the fetus to grow to its full size. If the egg attaches in such a way that the uterus has difficulty expanding to accept it, the uterus may start premature labor.

Asherman's Syndrome: A previous D & C, abortion, or infection can trigger a condition called Asherman's Syndrome, in which the scraping of the uterine wall causes adhesions. In healing, the walls of the uterus actually grow back together. A D & C can reopen the uterus, an outpatient procedure from which you will take four days to a week to recover.

Retroverted or Tilted Uterus: Some women have a uterus which tips back toward the rectum. Often this does not create problems because, in the first part of the pregnancy, the uterus returns to a normal position. In cases in which this does not occur, the fetus can be squeezed for room as it grows, and the uterus, assuming there is insufficient room, signals a miscarriage.

This condition can be diagnosed and you and your health care professional can do things to help the uterus position itself correctly. You can sleep on your stomach, a technique which sometimes persuades the uterus to return to a normal alignment. If this does not work, your health care provider can insert a pessary into the vagina to correct the tilt. This instrument supports the uterus and helps keep it in a normal position.

A tilted uterus can be discovered before conception in a normal doctor's appointment with a physical examination. Knowing ahead of time will allow you and your health care provider to take adequate precautions to resolve the situation. If a health care provider has ever suggested you had a tilted uterus, mention this to your health care professional early in your prenatal care.

Septate Uterus: Some women have a thin membrane that divides their uterus into two smaller chambers. This septum can inhibit the growth of a fetus and cause miscarriage. Discovered by laparoscopy or a hystosalpingogram, the septum can usually be removed easily.

Cervical Problems

The cervix, which lies at the bottom of the uterus, is a doughnut-shaped muscle that closes the uterus. When the uterus begins the contractions of labor to push the baby out of the uterus into the vagina to be delivered, the cervix thins out (effaces), creating an opening large enough for the baby to squeeze through. This dilation normally occurs only at delivery, but problems can occur when the cervix has been injured from previous medical procedures. The cervix can also have inherent abnormalities which leave it unable to bear the weight of the fetus and the amniotic sack. In these cases, the cervix dilates prematurely, causing the delivery of the baby long before it has developed enough to survive out of the womb.

Incompetent Cervix: The cervix can be weakened by previous medical procedures such as a D & C or even a previous delivery so that after fourteen weeks, when the weight of the developing fetus and the amniotic sack push upon the cervix, it dilates, causing a miscarriage. If you have recurrent second trimester miscarriages, an incompetent cervix is a possible cause. Your doctor can diagnose the problem if she or he discovers the cervix somewhat dilated early in the second trimester. Using a procedure called cervical cerclage, your health care provider closes off the cervix with sutures, stitching high on the cervix to lock the fetus safely in the uterus. For a vaginal delivery, the stitches are removed at about 38 weeks, or when labor begins.

Weakened Cervix from Cervical Cone Biopsy: The cervix can be weakened when the tissue sample necessary for a cone biopsy is taken. Stitching the cervix closed with a cervical cerclage is a successful solution to this problem.

Immunological Disorders

The body protects itself with a system that attacks anything it perceives as foreign. In the case of a pregnancy, the body normally blocks the immune system to protect the fetus, which the body would otherwise target as foreign. There is a great deal of interest in the immune system as a field that may provide answers to women who have had a number of undiagnosed miscarriages.

Stillbirth

Fetal death in the second and third trimester exacts a terrible toll on parents. If the baby has started to move around, kicking at certain times of the day or rollicking in the middle of the night, it has asserted itself enough to become a personality. By now the parents have seen her or his shape silhouetted on the sonogram, names may have been chosen, and both mother and father are emotionally invested in the outcome of the pregnancy.

Often the mother realizes there is something wrong, that the baby no longer seems to move, that all motion has ceased. As mentioned earlier, if the baby is dead, the parents can wait until the mother naturally begins labor, or they can decide to have labor induced.

Umbilical Cord Accidents

Sometimes late in the pregnancy the baby turns vigorously within the uterus, and these twists and turns can entangle the baby in the umbilical cord. The umbilical cord can also become knotted, preventing the flow of nourishment and oxygen to the baby. The cord itself can have blockages and aneurysms. A blocked cord fails to provide the essential nourishment and oxygen to the fetus. Gradual quieting of the fetus in the uterus can be a danger signal, and you must alert your doctor immediately. An ultrasound may reveal umbilical cord problems.

If your baby is stillborn, an autopsy may help to diagnose this problem.

What a Mother Can Do

When your baby dies, it is difficult not to blame yourself. The medical community has recognized certain factors leading to miscarriage, such as excessive alcohol, drug abuse, or cigarette smoking. On the whole, a mother is unable to help her unborn baby other than by eating well, consulting health care professionals and following their recommendations for prenatal care, and generally taking care of herself with rest, relaxation, and good nutrition. You need to reassure yourself that, unless there were unusual circumstances, nothing you could have done would increase your baby's chances of survival.

Sex During Pregnancy

Having sexual intercourse does not in any way affect a normal pregnancy. When spotting occurs after intercourse, you may worry that your baby was affected by you and the father having sex, but this is not the case. Sometimes spotting occurs just after intercourse because the cervix is softened from the pregnancy; this has nothing to do with miscarriage.

Miscarriage and Infertility

If you have had a miscarriage, the experience can seem devastating, but you can remain optimistic because you have proved you can conceive. However, for many women with a variety of reproductive problems, and for the fathers with male reproductive abnormalities, miscarriage of a baby they have tried for years to conceive can cause a plunge into despair.

Miscarriage has become more and more linked with infertility. Although all the factors for this are not clear, scientists ascribe the cause of increased infertility partly to delayed childbirth and environmental factors. Women are born with the total number of eggs they can produce already in place. As they begin to menstruate, usually at twelve or thirteen, the eggs begin to emerge. Over the entire span of a woman's reproductive life, the pattern continues. The older the eggs (for a 38-year-old woman, the eggs will be 38 years old), the greater the chance that the egg will not be viable. Even if fertilized by a sperm, an inviable egg will not implant in the uterine wall.

Men produce sperm throughout their lifetimes, but as they become older, the sperm have a greater risk of chromosomal abnormalities, and illness and infections can inhibit the quality and quantity of the sperm. Environmental factors such as pollution and chemicals from our foods may be affecting the quantity of sperm in men's ejaculate. Recent studies have shown a decline in the sperm count of ejaculate when compared to a study from the 1970s.

Infertility can plague a couple trying desperately to become pregnant. Surgery on both the man and the woman can improve their chances, but surgery for either is financially exhausting and physically demanding. All the problems of a miscarriage are exacerbated if the couple has rarely or never been able to become pregnant.

If you miscarry in your thirties, do not hesitate to define yourself as a mother with a high-risk pregnancy. Most women, young and old, who have had one miscarriage advocate not waiting for the medical standard of three miscarriages before trying to find out what is going wrong. When you define yourself high-risk, take steps to ensure your health and future. Because you are going against traditional medical practice, you may be labeled as hysterical or overreactive, but women who have more than three miscarriages risk permanent damage to their reproductive organs and further hazard to their fertility. Check with your insurance company, because many will not pay for testing until a woman has had more than three miscarriages.

If your health care professional does not take your concerns seriously, consider switching to another practitioner or consult a specialist. (See Chapter 4.)

There are a battery of tests you and the father can take to rule out certain physiological traits which may be inhibiting fertility and causing miscarriage. Some of the simplest and least invasive but equally important are tests to determine the viability and motility of the father's sperm. Discuss these issues with your health care practitioner, and ask for a consultation with a high-risk pregnancy specialist or an infertility counselor.

As you have read, there are many, many things that can go wrong physically to cause the end of your pregnancy and the death of your baby. When you have had a miscarriage, you want to try to find out what went wrong so you can feel that you have a better chance the next time. As an educated patient, you will know the danger signals of a pending miscarriage, and you can describe your symptoms to your health care professional. Early intervention with drugs or appropriate medical procedures may save the life of your baby when you know what went wrong the first time.

You must still face the fact that you may never know why your baby died. Even with all the scientific advances made in the last ten years, the practice of medicine is still inexact, and the intricate processes of reproducing life remain a mystery. Having a clear understanding of what might have gone wrong should help you understand that your feelings of grief, although unavoidable, are normal, and you are not to blame for the death of your baby. Although you can do very little to stop a miscarriage, you can plan for the future, and your preconception planning can help you bring your next baby to full term.

Questions to Ask Yourself

1. What symptoms did I notice before the miscarriage began?
2. Do I or the baby's father have any family medical history that may have caused this miscarriage?
3. Am I ready to talk, visit, return to my schedule or work, or do I need more to recover physically and emotionally?

4. Am I a mother with a high risk of miscarriage?
5. Do I and the father have a fertility problem?

Actions to Take

1. Try to find out why you miscarried. Make a written record of your pregnancy and everything you remember about it from the moment you knew you were pregnant. Note all your physical symptoms. Make a list of all your questions about your miscarriage and take it with you when you go to your next medical appointment.
2. Although it may be difficult, ask your mother and your mother-in-law whether they suffered any miscarriages or know of other family members who did.
3. Discuss with you health care professional the appropriate tests you and the father can take before your next pregnancy to diagnose any possible medical problems. Define a course of preconception testing and medical care for you and the father.
4. Create a team with yourself, the father, and your medical practitioner to work together for the next successful pregnancy. Read up on miscarriage and go to a medical library to look over the latest tests, procedures, and alternate treatments; then discuss your findings with the father and your health care provider.
5. Consult a genetic counselor for blood testing that will show any genetic abnormalities or incompatibilities in you or the father that may cause miscarriages early or late in the pregnancy.

Benediction

*May those of you whose unborn child dies be
granted the right to grieve until you find the
peace that eases pain.*

*May those of you who have suffered the death of
your child bear the pain of grief blessed by the
surrounding love of your family and friends.*

*May those of you who wish to have another baby
be blessed with the birth of a healthy child.*

*May those of you who face childlessness find a
choice to bring you happiness.*

*May those who bring another couple's child into
their lives experience the contentment of all
parents, accepting the attending joys and
sadnesses all parents know.*

*May those who accept childlessness find the
understanding to be the dispassionate elders
who guide children into the wisdom they
cannot accept from their own parents.*

Benediction

Appendix 1

Resources

The following organizations can provide you with information regarding miscarriage and infertility, and direct you to local organizations and services in your area.

American College of Obstetricians and Gynecologists
600 Maryland Avenue S.W., Suite 30
Washington, DC 20024
(202) 638-5577

American Fertility Society
1608 13th Avenue South, Suite 101
Birmingham, Al 35256

The Barren Foundation
60 East Monroe Street
Chicago, IL 60603

Center for Communications in Infertility, Inc.
P.O. Box 515
Yorktown, Heights, NY 10598

The Ferre Institute, Inc.
258 Genesee Street, Suite 302
Utica, NY 13502
Listings of infertility support groups, a resource library, a
newsletter, and informational brochures.

March of Dimes
1275 Mamaroneck Avenue
White Plains, NY 10605
(914) 428-7100

National Genetics Foundation
555 West 57th Street
New York, NY 10019

Planned Parenthood Western Region
333 Broadway, 3rd Floor
San Francisco, CA 94133
(415) 956-8856
General counseling services.

Planned Parenthood Federation of America
810 Seventh Avenue
New York, NY 10019
(212) 541-7800
General counseling services.

RESOLVE
P.O. Box 474
Belmont, MA 02178
(617) 643-2424
Miscarriage and infertility counseling services and
referral.

Appendix 2

Medical Preparation for Subsequent Pregnancy

Fifteen to twenty percent of clinically recognized pregnancies are lost. The causes of pregnancy loss are numerous. The chance for a successful pregnancy following one loss is 76%; following two losses, 74%. In order to increase your chances of success following pregnancy loss, some of the procedures shown in the chart on the next two pages may be done (one or all in any category).

The following chart is reprinted by permission of the Ferre Institute, Inc.

Causes of Pregnancy Loss	Procedures Following Loss
Anatomical	
• Malformation of uterus—e.g., T-shaped uterus or septum (wall) in uterus • Incompetent cervix • Uterine fibroids • Adhesions (scar tissue) inside uterus	• Hysterosalpingogram • Hysteroscopy • Sonogram • Laparoscopy
Hormonal	
• Inadequate amount of progesterone—luteal phase defect • Abnormal function of other hormones secreting organs, e.g., thyroid, adrenal, pituitary	• Blood hormone tests • Basal body temperature graph • Endometrial biopsy
Teratogens Teratogens are agents that can interfere with normal embryo/fetus development.	
• Significant X-ray exposure • Chemical exposure at work or at home • Drug exposure—prescription and non-prescription • Alcohol and substance abuse • Infectious agents—rubella, toxoplasmosis, cytomegalovirus, herpes, hepatitis, T-mycoplasm	• Report known exposure history to physician • Blood tests for exposure to infectious agents
Maternal Factors	
• Mothers with medical conditions such as diabetes mellitus, lupus, seizure disorders may be more prone to pregnancy loss. • Maternal infection with T-mycoplasm • Maternal age of 35 years and older can increase risk of pregnancy loss	• Accurate diagnosis of medical condition • Careful monitoring or medications in future pregnancy

Paternal Factors	• Paternal infection with T-mycoplasm • Workplace exposures	• Accurate diagnosis of any medical condition or infection • Careful consideration of workplace exposures
Immunological	• Maternal immune system unable to protect fetus from (tissue) rejection	• HLA or ANA blood testing
Genetic/Chromosome Abnormality	• The majority (50–60%) of early pregnancy loss (less than 12 weeks) is due to an abnormal chromosome composition. Every cell requires 46 intact chromosomes to allow for normal development. Change in chromosome number or individual chromosome constitution can increase risk for miscarriage. Most errors in chromosome number or constitution are accidental. Occasionally *inherited* (from either parent) chromosome rearrangements predispose one to miscarriage.	• Blood chromosome testing (in cases of suspected inherited abnormalities)
Placenta & Cord	• Placenta abruptio—premature separation of placenta • Placenta previa—placenta is overlapping the cervix • Placental infection • Knot in cord • Cord wrapped around fetus	• Careful exam of placenta and cord • Review sonograms
Pre-term Labor	• Premature onset of labor (6–10% of all births are pre-term)	• Examination for general medical conditions

Glossary

This glossary defines terms used in this book and in other sources about miscarriage. Use it to look up unfamiliar terms you read or hear from health care professionals.

A

abortion: Pregnancy termination, either spontaneously by a woman's body or through medical intervention (therapeutic).

abortus: The medical term for a fetus lost in miscarriage or abortion.

abruptio placentae: See *placenta abruptio.*

acrosin: An enzyme in the head of the sperm that assists in penetrating the egg (ova).

acrosome: A cap contained in the head of the sperm that holds the acrosin.

ACTH: See *adrenocorticotropic hormone.*

acute salpingitis: An inflammation of the fallopian tube caused by an infection.

adenoma: A benign tumor, usually small.

adhesions: Scar tissue created by the body as a response to inflammation, infections or other diseases, or surgery.

adrenocorticotropic hormone (ACTH): A pituitary hormone that causes the adrenal gland to release cortisol hormone.

agglutinization: When two or more sperm clump together.

AID: See *artificial insemination by donor.*

AIH: See *artificial insemination by husband.*

alpha fetal protein test: Usually performed at 16 weeks, this blood test monitors the amount of alpha fetal protein produced by the fetus, which normally increases through-out the pregnancy. Too high amounts may indicate neural tube defects such as spina bifida or anencephaly, or may indicate multiple births. This is a controversial test with a risk of inaccuracy; a second test is usually ordered if the first turns out abnormal. Doctors check the results with ultrasound. Amniocentesis is used as a final verification of neural tube defects.

amenorrhea: When menstruation cycles are absent.

amenorrhea galactorrhea: When menstruation cycles are absent but milk is present in the breasts.

amniocentesis: Usually performed from fifteen to eighteen weeks, this test of the amniotic fluid provides cells that are cultured and analyzed for a variety of fetal defects, infection, and fetal lung development. Using a local anesthetic, the doctor inserts a thin needle through the mother's abdomen and into the amniotic sac, withdrawing a small amount of fluid for culturing. Guided by ultrasound, the doctor can clearly direct the needle to avoid injury to the fetus. This test carries some risk to the fetus and should be undertaken when the mother falls into a high-risk group for fetal defects.

amniotic sac: A sac of thin membrane filled with watery fluid in the mother's uterus in which the fetus grows and develops.

androgens: Male hormones produced by both men and women.

andrologist: A urologist with a specialty in male reproductive problems.

andrology: The medical study of the male reproductive system.

anesthesia: The use of drugs to control and diminish pain.

anovulation: When ovulation does not occur.

anoxia: Fetal death that is a result of cutting off the oxygen supply, most often from umbilical cord or placental problems.

artificial insemination by donor (AID): Sperm from a donor male is inserted with a syringe into the vagina or uterus of a fertile woman to fertilize her egg. This procedure is used to overcome low sperm count, sperm motility problems, sperm antibodies, or cervical mucus problems.

artificial insemination by husband (AIH): When sperm from a husband is inserted with a syringe into the vagina or uterus of his wife to fertilize the egg. This procedure is used to overcome low sperm count, sperm motility problems, sperm antibodies, or cervical mucus problems.

asthenospermia: When less than half of the sperm in a man's ejaculate do not swim properly, and consequently the male is diagnosed as having sperm motility problems.

atretic process: Women are born with 1–2 million immature ovarian follicles called oocytes. Their normal and gradual disintegration over a woman's fertile life span is called the atretic process. When women begin menstruation, the remaining viable follicles will ovulate over 400 eggs.

autoimmune antibodies: Antibodies produced by a woman's body that interfere with the normal growth of the fetus and cause miscarriage.

azoospermia: When testing reveals no sperm in the ejaculate.

B

basal body temperature (BBT) chart: A record of the woman's temperature taken each morning before any activity. Temperatures are lower before ovulation and higher afterward. BBT charts are one means to determine when a woman is ovulating.

bicornate uterus: When the uterus is divided either partially or totally into two parts by a tissue membrane. This unusual condition sometimes occurs in women whose mothers took DES during their pregnancies.

biophysical profiles: Ultrasound exams used later in pregnancy to check the fetal heart function and fetal movement.

biopsy: A medical procedure in which a small amount of tissue is removed for cell analysis.

birth control pills: Synthetic female hormones used to correct menstrual cycles, prohibit contraception, or treat conditions such as endometriosis.

blighted ovum: A fertilized egg in which development has stopped.

bovine cervical mucus test: A test that determines whether the male sperm can penetrate cervical mucus. The test is used to check male fertility.

bromocriptine (Parlodel): The female body produces a hormone called prolactin which can, when elevated, produce irregular ovulation. Bromocriptine is a drug that regulates the amount of prolactin produced by the body.

C

capacitation: As the sperm works its way through the fallopian tubes to reach an egg, the cap of the sperm wears away, allowing the release of certain enzymes that enable the sperm to finally penetrate the egg.

CAT scan: An X-ray that creates a computer-generated image of the interior of the body.

caudal anesthesia: An anesthetic injected in the air spaces around the spinal column to produce a numbing of the legs and pelvic area.

cervical cerclage: A procedure in which a prematurely dilated cervix is closed off with sutures in order to lock the fetus safely in the uterus.

cervical mucus: The cervix produces a mucus which changes character throughout the menstrual cycle and can be favorable or hostile to the passage of the sperm.

cervix: The narrow opening that connects the uterus and the vagina. The cervix holds the fetus in the uterus during pregnancy, and expands during delivery to let the fetus through to the birth canal. An improperly functioning cervix can lead to miscarriage. See *incompetent cervix.*

cesarean birth: When a baby is delivered surgically through the abdominal wall.

chlamydia: A sexually transmitted disease caused by a bacterium Chlamydea trachomatis that some researchers believe is responsible for miscarriage and premature birth. Symptoms are barely recognizable, such as a yellowish discharge, abdominal pain, and sometimes slight bleeding during intercourse. A woman who may have been exposed should ask to be tested either before pregnancy or in the early months. The disease can be successfully treated with antibiotics.

chocolate cysts: Sometimes also called endometriomas, these ovarian cysts are caused by endometriosis.

chromosome: In the body cell, the nucleus contains chromosomes, each one carrying the parent's genetic makeup.

chronic salpingitis: Scarring or blockages on the fallopian tubes caused by infection.

chorionic villus sampling (CVS): A test used to discover chromosomal and biochemical abnormalities in the fetus, as well as the baby's sex. A sample of the chorionic villi—the developing placenta—is collected with a thin tube inserted into the uterus with the aid of ultrasound. The test is usually performed ten to twelve weeks after conception. There is some chance of infection from the procedure and subsequent risk of miscarriage.

cilia: Small projections in the fallopian tubes, almost like hairs, which help to push the ovum toward the uterus.

clitoris: The sexual organ in a woman composed of erectile tissue, sensitive to physical stimulation leading to orgasm.

clomid, clomiphene citrate (Serophene or Clomid): A fertility drug that brings on ovulation. Some women experience physical symptoms of nausea, breast tenderness, hot flashes, vision problems, as well as emotional sensitivity. The standard dose is one 50 mg pill a day for five days.

complete abortion: When the body rejects all fetal and placental tissue after a miscarriage, making medical intervention unnecessary.

conception: When a sperm fertilizes an egg.

congenital: A description of a condition existing in a baby at birth, such as a congenital birth defect.

corpus luteum: From the Latin term meaning yellow body, this is the transformed follicle (the follicle after it has released the egg) that regulates the hormones, allowing for successful implantation of the egg in the uterus.

culture of fetal tissues: The process in which tissue is grown in the laboratory to discover whether infections were responsible for miscarriage.

culture of the vagina and uterus: Women prone to uterine infections should be cultured after a miscarriage to determine whether an infection was responsible. The process is also used during subsequent pregnancies to monitor infection.

curettage: See *dilation and curettage.*

D

danozol (Danocrine): A drug synthesized from male hormones to treat endometriosis. The hormone stops the fluctuating hormonal patterns that create ovulation and menstruation. Side effects may be increased facial hair, lower voice timbre, and weight gain. After four to eight months, women try to become pregnant.

Diethylstilbestrol (DES): A drug widely prescribed to women from 1941 to 1971—until it was discovered to cause birth defects—in order to prevent miscarriage. Men and women whose mother took the drug run an increased risk of cancer or may have defects in their reproductive organs that affect their fertility.

dilation and curettage (D & C): This medical procedure, done under anesthesia, cleans the interior of the uterus and is a necessary procedure after an incomplete abortion. The cervix is dilated either with a slowly swelling plug (laminaria) or through medication to insert the instrument which, rather like a miniature vacuum, removes all the remaining fetal tissue and uterine lining.

doppler: A hand-held ultrasound to detect fetal heartbeat beginning at six weeks.

duct obstruction: An obstruction or blockage in a man's vas deferens or epididymis.

dysmenorrhea: Menstruation with painful cramping and often including symptoms of nausea and diarrhea.

E

eclampsia: See *preeclampsia.*

ectopic pregnancy: For different reasons, an egg will implant outside the uterus, often in the fallopian tubes. Its growth in such places creates a life-threatening situation for the woman. Once this happens, there is no way to transplant the egg into the uterus. Surgery or miscarriage are certain outcomes.

ejaculate: The semen-filled liquid that is discharged by the male during climax.

embryo: The fertilized ovum is called an embryo from the time of conception up to the eighth week of pregnancy.

endocrine system: The system of glands that produces and releases hormones into the bloodstream.

endocrinologist: A medical specialist who deals with the endocrine system.

endometrial biopsy: A medical procedure in which a small piece of the endometrial lining is scraped away in order to test its maturity.

endometriomas: Cysts formed in the ovary by endometriosis.

endometriosis: A condition in which the endometrial cells that normally line the uterus implant and grow elsewhere.

endometrium: The uterine lining that sheds during menstruation or remains to become the host for the fertilized embryo.

epididymis: The duct system in which the sperm mature, developing the ability to fertilize the ovum.

epididymitis: An inflammation of the epididymis.

epididymovasostomy: Surgery to remove a blockage in the epididymis.

estrogen: A female hormone that is produced by the egg follicles as they develop to stimulate the uterine lining and make the cervical mucus amiable toward sperm.

F

fallopian tubes: A pair of tubes, one on each side of the uterus, through which the eggs travel from the ovary to the uterus. When a fertilized egg implants in the tube, it becomes the site of an ectopic pregnancy, which will be terminated through miscarriage, rupture of the tube if undetected, or through surgery when detected.

fertilization: When a sperm unites with an egg.

fetus: An embryo after the second month of gestation until birth.

fibroid tumors: Benign tumors in the uterus which can hinder a woman's fertility.

follicle-stimulating hormone (FSH): This hormone stimulates the production of sperm in men and eggs in women.

fructose test: A test that determines the level of sugar in a man's semen.

FSH: See *follicle-stimulating hormone.*

G

galactorrhea: Women producing a high amount of the hormone prolactin may produce breast milk without pregnancy. This abnormal condition needs medical attention to bring about a hormonal adjustment.

gamete intrafallopian tube transfer (GIFT): A procedure to increase fertility in which a woman's egg is removed, mixed with her partner's sperm, and then replaced along with the sperm in her fallopian tubes for natural fertilization.

genetics: From the word genesis, meaning the beginning of things. Genetics is the study of heredity and variation.

GIFT: See *gamete intrafallopian tube transfer.*

gonadotropin-releasing hormone (Gn RH): The hypothalamus releases this hormone, which causes the pituitary to release FSH and LH hormones (the hormones that regulate reproductive processes in men and women).

gonorrhea: A bacterial, sexually transmitted disease.

H

habitual aborter: A term, disliked by more progressive gynecologists, to describe women who have miscarried three or more times.

hamster egg test: A male fertility test in which the male's sperm is tested for effectiveness by its ability to penetrate an ovum of a hamster.

HCG: See *human chorionic gonadotropin.*

HELLP Syndrome: An acronym for "hemolysis, elevated liver enzymes, and low platelet count." This very serious medical complication occurs in conjunction with preeclampsia and abruptio placentae. It results in high maternal mortality, premature delivery (in order to save the mother's life), or subsequent medical complications for the infant. The incidence is higher in white women.

HLA tissue typing: A procedure that determines whether a mother's autoimmune system is threatening to the fetus, which may lead to multiple miscarriages.

HMG: See *human menopausal gonadotropin.*

hormones: The endocrine glands secrete these chemical compounds that in turn cause the secretion of other complex biochemical compounds.

Huhner's test (post-coital test/PCT): A test that shows how a women's cervical mucus interacts with her partner's sperm.

human chorionic gonadotropin (HCG): After conception, the placenta releases this hormone into the mother's bloodstream. In testing, its presence is a sure indication of pregnancy. There is a measurable rise of HCG throughout pregnancy, and levels that deviate from the norm may signal abnormalities in the pregnancy or multiple births.

human menopausal gonadotropin (HMG) (Pergonal): This drug, taken to increase fertility in women, is made from purified FSH and LH hormone, derived from the urine of post-menopausal women.

hyaluronidase: The enzyme in the head of the sperm that helps to break a path into the egg.

Hyperprolactinism: A condition indicated by testing that shows above normal amounts of prolactin hormone in the bloodstream.

hypothalamus: The part of the brain close to the pituitary gland that regulates the hormones secreted by the pituitary gland.

hysterectomy: Medical surgery that removes the uterus.

hysterosalpingogram (HSG): A procedure in which dye is pumped into the uterus through the vagina and then X-rayed to discover anatomical defects of the tubes and the uterus, as well as any growths such as cysts or fibroids.

hysteroscopy: A procedure in which a tiny telescope is inserted into the uterus.

I

ICSH: See *interstitial cell stimulating hormone.*

idiopathic oligospermia: When a male has a low sperm count for no known cause or traceable medical reason.

immobilization: When sperm do not move, or seemingly "attempt" to move, with no result.

immunobead binding test: Testing that searches for and pinpoints the presence and location of sperm antibodies on the sperm.

immunoglobulins: Proteins that circulate in the blood, and are part of the body's immune system.

immunological infertility: Infertility caused by either the male or female's immune system having a protective, and therefore hostile, response to the sperm.

implantation: When the zygote attaches to a wall lining, normally in the uterus, abnormally outside the uterus.

impotence: The inability of a man to achieve or sustain a penile erection.

incompetent cervix: Some cervix are too weak to support the weight of a growing fetus in the uterus, and as the fetus grows, the cervix flattens and expands as it does in childbirth, with the resulting loss of the pregnancy, usually after twelve or more weeks. A medical procedure called a cerclage can strengthen the cervix by stitching it closed until about thirty-seven weeks when the stitches are removed to allow normal childbirth.

incomplete abortion: A spontaneous abortion in which all the fetal tissue is not ejected by the body, allowing possible development of uterine infection from the tissue remaining in the uterus. A dilation and curettage ("D & C") is usually prescribed to protect the mother's health. A woman who suspects she has had a spontaneous abortion should be checked by her doctor to determine whether she should undergo a D & C.

infertility: When a woman has not been able to achieve or maintain pregnancy after one year of unprotected intercourse. Either the man or the woman may have a medical condition responsible for the infertility.

infertility specialist: A medical doctor, generally a gynecologist, specializing in the diagnosis and treatment of women (as well as their partners) who have been unable to become pregnant or maintain pregnancy.

inflammation: A physical response to infection through pain, tissue swelling, or permanent scarring.

intrauterine device (IUD): A contraceptive device inserted into the uterus to prevent a fertilized egg from implanting. This device may create fertility problems in some women because of the high rate of infection associated with its use.

in vitro fertilization (IVF): A method to induce pregnancy by extracting eggs from the mother and adding sperm from the father outside a woman's body. The fertilized eggs are then reinserted into the woman's uterus to begin the pregnancy.

in vivo fertilization: When an egg is naturally fertilized by a sperm inside a woman's body without medical intervention.

IUD: See *intrauterine device.*

IVF: See *in vitro fertilization.*

K

karyotyping: a chromosomal analysis of fetal tissue (conceptus) that detects chromosomal abnormalities.

Klinefelter's syndrome: A rare male disorder in which the father's chromosome carries an extra X chromosome.

L

laparoscopy: A procedure in which a small "telescope" is inserted through the abdomen wall near the navel in order to inspect all the reproductive organs.

laparotomy: Making an incision through the abdomen.

laser surgery: Using a laser beam for surgery, either by itself or in conjunction with other microsurgical techniques.

Leydig cells: Cells located inside the testes that produce the hormone testosterone.

LH: See *luteinizing hormone.*

local anesthesia: Injecting pain-numbing medication locally while the patient remains conscious.

luteal phase: One of two phases of menstruation. The luteal phase follows ovulation and continues until menstruation.

luteal phase defect: A condition in which the luteal phase is shortened or too little progesterone is produced during the phase. The absence of progesterone may affect the growth of the endometrial lining, with subsequent effects on fertility including possible miscarriage.

lutein: A yellow pigment manufactured from cholesterol.

luteinizing hormone (LH): A pituitary hormone that regulates ovulation and progesterone output in women and testosterone production in men.

M

Maternal Serum Alphafeto protein (MSAFP): A blood screening test that measures Alphafeto protein, produced by the fetus. The test is run between fifteen and eighteen weeks of pregnancy for high-risk women to identify any possible fetal abnormalities.

menarche: The first menstruation in a girl, usually occurring between nine and fourteen years of age.

menopause: A number of years of irregular periods and emotional mood-swings, occurring between 45 and 55 years of age. Menopause is said to be completed when menstruation has been totally absent for two years.

menstrual cycle: A woman's monthly cycle regulated by hormones to build up the endometrium, release an egg, and then to shed the endometrium. The cycle usually runs from 25 to 35 days.

menstruation: The shedding of the endometrium if a fertilized egg has not implanted.

missed abortion: When pregnancy ends with a miscarriage and all symptoms of pregnancy stop, but the body does not flush out all the fetal tissue.

molar pregnancy: An unusual and rare condition in which the placenta forms cysts and the embryo never develops.

motility: The ability of sperm to move forward so they can travel through the vagina and the uterus to fertilize an egg.

mycoplasma: A reproductive tract bacterial infection like chlamydia that can cause miscarriage. The infection has no outward symptoms to suggest diagnosis and treatment.

N

neonatal death: The death of a baby in the first month of its life outside the body.

neonatologist: A doctor who specializes in the care of newborn babies.

nidation: When a fertilized egg implants in the ovary.

O

obstetrician: A doctor specializing in the health of women's reproductive organs, pregnancy, and birth.

oligospermia: A condition in which a man's sperm count consistently stays below normal.

os: The cervical opening to the uterus.

ovaries: Reproduction organs in the woman in which the lifelong supply of eggs are stored and released. Ovaries also release the hormones estrogen and progesterone.

oviduct: An alternative name for a fallopian tube.

ovulation: When an ovum (egg) is released from the ovary.

ovulation induction: Medical intervention through the use of hormones to stimulate the ovary to release an egg.

ovum: An egg.

ovum transfer: When a fertilized egg is taken out of a donor and inserted into a recipient.

oxytocin challenge test: In this test, doctors inject a low dose of a synthetic hormone called oxytocin to mothers who have developed complications during the late stages of their pregnancy. The oxytocin induces a series of contractions, which "challenge" the fetus and allow doctors to monitor its condition. If the fetal heart rate drops after a contraction, the baby may be in danger, while a heart rate that remains stable indicates a healthy fetus that may continue uterine development.

P

PAP smear test: A medical test that examines a smear of cervical cells to detect any cellular abnormalities.

pelvic inflammatory disease (PID): Infections of the female reproductive organs, which can produce scarring that inhibits fertility or more serious illness.

PID: See *pelvic inflammatory disease.*

pituitary gland: One of a system of glands that regulate body processes by releasing hormones directly into the bloodstream. The pituitary, hypothalamus, and sex glands work in unison to orchestrate sperm production, ovulation, and early pregnancy through the release of estrogen, progesterone, prolactin, and testosterone—sex hormones essential to both men and women.

placenta: The placenta, shaped like a disk, is the connection to the uterine wall of the umbilical cord. The tissue connects the mother and fetus and provides nourishment to the fetus as well as taking away the waste. It is delivered after the birth of a baby, and is consequently known as the afterbirth.

placenta abruptio: If the placenta partially tears away from the uterine wall, the developing fetus is deprived of both oxygen and nutrients. When the placenta separates, the mother will feel sharp pain and begin to bleed. Placenta abruptio usually occurs in the third trimester and may result in fetal death.

placenta previa: If the placenta fixes itself over the mouth of the cervix instead of high up on the uterine wall, childbirth will force the placenta to deliver first, cutting off oxygen to the fetus and possibly leading to fetal death.

polycystic ovarian syndrome (PCO): Also called Stein-Leventhal syndrome, PCO describes a condition in which cysts form on the ovaries in response to hormonal imbalances that disrupt the ovulation process.

post-birth control pill syndrome: Birth control pills disrupt normal ovulation by keeping the pituitary and hypothalamus glands from producing the hormones that guide ovulation. Women who have had ovulatory problems prior to taking oral contraceptives may find that ovulation does not occur after taking birth control pills; other women may take from three to twelve months to resume ovulation.

prednisone: A steroid drug sometimes prescribed to prevent immune disorders that can cause miscarriage.

preeclampsia (toxemia): A serious medical emergency which becomes eclampsia, a state in which the woman's body undergoes critical shutdown of the vital organs including a reduction in total blood volume. The treatment for severe preeclampsia is immediate delivery of the baby.

premature ovarian failure: An irreversible condition in which the ovary stops producing eggs before menopause. Doctors diagnose this condition through a physical examination and lab tests. Women under 30 years of age can be tested through karyotyping. Some doctors may recommend estrogen to prevent osteoporosis and atrophy of the genital tract.

progesterone: Usually secreted during the luteal phase of menstruation, normal levels of this hormone are critical to successful pregnancy, and insufficient levels may lead to miscarriage. Spotting, bleeding, or cramps during pregnancy may indicate an insufficient supply of progesterone.

prolactin: A hormone released by the pituitary gland that stimulates lactation.

proliferative phase: The first half of the menstruation cycle, ending in ovulation.

prostaglandins: Hormones that induce uterine contractions before menstruation or during the labor of childbirth.

prostrate gland: A man's reproductive gland that produces the seminal liquid to the sperm before ejaculation.

R

RESOLVE: A national network of groups to support women who have experienced miscarriage and to educate health professionals regarding miscarriage.

retrograde ejaculation: An abnormal condition in which a man's sperm is ejaculated into his bladder.

Rh immunoglobulin (RhIg): A medication used to prevent an Rh-negative person's antibody to Rh-positive blood cells.

ritodrine: A medication used to stop early contractions.

S

salpingitis: A condition in which the fallopian tubes have become scarred, blocked, or closed from pelvic inflammatory diseases (such as gonorrhea, infections from intrauterine devices, or other diseases). Acute salpingitis is the term for active infection.

secondary amenorrhea: A condition in which menstruation lapses for three or more consecutive periods.

secondary infertility: When a woman who has had one or more successful pregnancies is unable to bring another pregnancy full term.

secretory cells: Fluid-producing cells inside the fallopian tubes.

semen: The thick fluid men ejaculate during climax that contains seminal fluid and sperm.

semen analysis: A test that analyzes semen for sperm count, motility, morphology, and other characteristics in order to judge the ability of the sperm to fertilize an egg.

seminal vesicles: The glands in a man which store sperm and produce the semen.

seminiferous tubules: Sperm-producing tubes within the testes.

septate uterus: When a wall or membrane of the uterus protrudes into the uterine cavity. It often causes miscarriage, since the divided uterus is too small to hold a growing fetus. A surgical procedure removes the membrane.

serum beta HCG test: A simple blood test that measures human chorionic gonadotropin to determine pregnancy and the progression of the pregnancy. A lower than normal reading can indicate ectopic pregnancy, fetal death, or nonviable pregnancy. A higher than normal reading can indicate multiple births or a molar pregnancy.

serum progesterone test: A blood test drawn after ovulation to test the progesterone levels.

sperm: The male germ cells released during climax that contain genetic information. When sperm penetrate a woman's egg, fertilization occurs.

sperm antibodies: Antibodies produced by both men and women's natural defense systems that can damage or destroy sperm.

sperm bank: A special clinic that collects, freezes, and stores sperm for use in artificial insemination.

sperm count: An estimate of the number of sperm in the semen. A low sperm count may indicate medical problems or cause infertility.

sperm penetration assay: A test of male fertility in which a sperm is analyzed for its ability to penetrate a hamster egg.

sperm washing: A special technique that separates the sperm from the semen.

spermatic cord: The tube along which the sperm travels from the testicle to the urethra for ejaculation.

spermatogenesis: The process by which a man produces sperm.

spinal anesthesia: An injection of pain-numbing medication into the spinal canal. This type of injection is often used in childbirth to numb the body below the waist.

spontaneous abortion: The medical term for a miscarriage, usually occurring during the first or second trimester.

STD: A sexually transmitted disease.

Stein-Leventhal syndrome: See *polycystic ovarian syndrome.*

sterility: Infertility which has been diagnosed as permanent and untreatable.

stillbirth: The death of a fetus after the twentieth week of pregnancy.

superovulation: A method of implanting several eggs in the uterus, often used in in vitro fertilization.

syphilis: A sexually transmitted disease that is treatable with antibiotics. Pregnant women with syphilis have a 50 percent change of losing their baby before birth. If the baby is born, it will be infected. Most doctors screen pregnant women for this disease.

T

T-mycoplasma: A microorganism that can cause miscarriage or premature birth. There are no symptoms except repeated miscarriages—seemingly without cause. If diagnosed, it can be treated with antibiotics.

testicle: A man's reproductive organs that produce sperm and male hormones. Two testicles are enclosed in a scrotum, a sack-like pouch that hangs down behind the penis. A man produces sperm all his life, although illness or age may decrease the amount and viability of sperm.

testicular biopsy: A procedure done under anesthesia to remove a tissue sample from the testicle for testing.

testosterone: A male hormone manufactured in the testes throughout a man's life that affects sexual drive.

threatened abortion: Danger signals to pregnant women—menstrual-type spotting, bleeding, and cramping—that may indicate a spontaneous abortion.

thyroid: The endocrine gland that produces thyroxin hormone which regulates the body's growth and metabolism.

toxemia: A complication usually occurring in the last months of pregnancy with symptoms of elevated blood pressure, swelling of the ankles or other extremities, and protein in the urine.

tubal patency: A tube with no indication of blockage or decreased ability to function fully.

U

ultrasound: High frequency sound waves that create a picture on a monitor enabling the health professional to follow the growth and development of a fetus. Both abdominal and vaginal ultrasound are available, but vaginal ultrasound produces clearer pictures. Abdominal ultrasound may be more uncomfortable because it requires that the patient have a full bladder throughout the procedure.

unexplained infertility: A diagnosis indicating no medical explanation for a couple's inability to become pregnant.

urethra: The tube through which both urine and semen travel through the penis, but not simultaneously.

urologist: A doctor specializing in male or female reproductive problems, including urinary tract diseases and infertility.

uterus: A woman's reproductive organ which, when she is not pregnant, becomes lined with endometrium monthly. After a successful implantation of a fertilized egg, it is the womb for the developing fetus.

V

vagina: The muscular tunnel between the cervix and the vulva that becomes the birth canal.

vaginal suppository: A solid cone of medicated material that melts when inserted into the vagina, allowing a gradual distribution of the medication.

vas deferens: The long tubes that connect the seminal vesicles to the epididymis. The sperm are transported through the vas deferens by a series of contractions for up to 10 to 14 days, during which they become both fertile and able to move through the vigorous flagellation of the tail of the sperm. There is one vas deferens for each testicle.

vasectomy: A medical procedure in which both vas deferens are cut to prohibit sperm being transported to the epididymis, thereby assuring the sterility of the man.

vasectomy reversal: A medical procedure that reconnects the vas deferens, allowing sperm to flow into the epididymis and thereby assuring male fertility. This procedure is not always successful.

vasography: An X-ray of the vas deferens.

Z

zona pellucida: The outer covering of the ovum. The sperm produces a special enzyme that helps to dissolve the covering and allow entry of the sperm.

zygote: An egg successfully fertilized by a sperm. Once fertilized, the zygote begins the process of cell division. After three divisions and several days, the eight-cell zygote migrates to the uterus where, with successful implantation, it begins to produce the HCG hormone that regulates the corpus luteum's production of progesterone and estrogen.

References

The Boston Women's Health Collective. *The New Bodies, Ourselves: A Book by and for Women.* New York: Touchstone, Simon & Schuster, 1992.

Liebmann-Smith, Joan. *In Pursuit of Pregnancy. How Couples Discover, Cope with, and Resolve Their Fertility Problems.* New York: Newmarket, 1987.

Sanders, Catherine M., Ph.D. *How to Survive the Loss of a Child: Filling the Emptiness and Rebuilding Your Life.* Rocklin, CA: Prima Publishing, 1992.

Senchyshyn, Stefan, M.D., and Carol Colman. *How to Prevent Miscarriage and Other Crises of Pregnancy: A Leading High-Risk Pregnancy Doctor's Prescription for Carrying Your Baby to Term.* New York: Collier Books, 1990.

Stangel, John J., M.D. *Fertility and Conception, an Essential Guide for Childless Couples.* New York: Paddington, 1979.

Index